Food
for
Life

food *for* life

michelle bridges

Pan Macmillan Australia

CONTENTS

INTRODUCTION

I've been working in the health and fitness industry for a long time and it's been an amazing journey. Through my online 12 Week Body Transformation, my work on *The Biggest Loser* and all of my books, I've helped thousands of people shift their thinking about diet and exercise so that they become the best versions of themselves they can be. And I love what I do. I love seeing people taking control of their lives, empowering themselves to make positive change.

Physical fitness is my passion, so exercise has always formed a major part of my healthy weight-loss programs and, let's face it, exercise is non-negotiable when it comes to losing a *lot* of weight. It's also important for mental health: studies show it can improve your mood, boost your concentration and alertness, and even help you develop a more optimistic way of looking at the world, all of which influence your mindset and eating habits. Personally, I can't imagine my life without exercise; I just feel so good when I move! Yet, I've always maintained that you can't outrun a bad diet – that what you eat has a far greater influence on your weight and health than exercise alone.

Without a doubt, DIET is the number-one factor in WEIGHT LOSS.

Without a doubt, diet is the number-one factor in weight loss. Even with all the training in the world, if you eat sugary, fatty processed food, you are going to put on weight. Conversely, eating the right foods in the right amounts will mean you maintain a healthy weight or lose weight (if you have weight to lose). Not only that, it will contribute to your overall health and wellbeing. Certain nutrients can help us to ward off disease, live longer lives, boost cognitive power, ensure optimal operation of our physiological functions and improve our mood.

Now, I'm not saying that you should eat lettuce and sit on the couch for the rest of your life – exercise is still critical for a whole range of reasons, not least of which is being able to step out of the shower without breaking your hip when you're over 60 – but if you understand a little bit more about how what you eat affects your body, I know that it will inspire you to make healthier food choices. And this is key: what you eat is *your* choice.

It sounds so easy, doesn't it? Yet what we choose to eat depends on a stack of complex and interrelated factors, including the eating patterns we learned in childhood; the prevalence of cheap fast food; our consumer lifestyle (bigger, better, faster, more – 'I want it all and I want it now'); aggressive marketing by the big food giants; aisles of crap food in supermarkets; our ethical principles (whether we eat animals, sustainable food, biodynamic or organic food), and, most importantly, our stress levels and emotional state.

When we feel anxious or depressed, many of us look to food (especially sugary or fatty foods) to make us feel better. And there is a biological reason for this. Sweet foods activate the reward pathways in our brains ('This is GREAT! Gimme more!'), which makes sense because our brains run on glucose and we need it for all of our bodily functions. However, when we have too much sugar, it not only gets stored as fat (hello heart disease), it also messes with our insulin levels (insulin resistance), which can lead to type 2 diabetes – I talk more about this on page 9.

Fats are a bit different. We still love the soothing and satisfying feeling we get when we eat high-energy foods like nuts, avocado, coconut, dairy foods and animal protein, but because our bodies have evolved an 'off switch' (the energy-balancing hormone leptin) to tell our brains that we've had enough fat, it's harder to eat too much of it. Unfortunately, if we are already overweight or obese, our appetite-controlling hormones are already out of whack, and the messages that we've stored enough fat are not getting through.

> ### The most lethal combo is FAT and SUGAR, which happens to be present in pretty much every PROCESSED FOOD you can buy.

Of course, the most lethal combo is fat *and* sugar, which happens to be present in pretty much every processed food you can buy – chocolate, ice cream, cake, pastries, biscuits, spreads, dressings, sauces, even crackers and bread.

Now, I could give you a whole bunch of scary statistics about the connection between obesity, diabetes and heart disease, and how many of us are playing with fire when we eat so much processed food, but that's not going to help you make better food choices. I know from experience that long-lasting change won't come from fear. It has to come from a place of acceptance. You will only care about what you eat when you care about yourself. This amazing collection of molecules and particles that makes up your body is uniquely yours, and you have the opportunity to look after it, nourish it and honour it any way you choose. I'm inviting you to put your health first because it all starts and ends with you.

I often hear *The Biggest Loser* contestants standing on the scales telling the world they need to lose weight and they're doing it 'for my kids' or 'for my husband'. While their hearts are in the right place, their minds are not. Other people's happiness is not your responsibility. In any case, you will always be better able to look after others when you have taken the trouble to look after yourself. How can you take care of your kids if you're chronically unwell yourself? Or enjoy your grandchildren if you're constantly in and out of hospital? Or support your family if you're too sick to work?

For me, food is nourishment for the BODY and MIND.

For me, food is nourishment for the body and mind. It's also a celebration of the little pleasures that make up a happy life – the aroma of basil freshly picked from the herb garden, the vibrant colour of a freshly tossed salad, the joy you feel when your family or friends tell you how much they love your cooking. All too often I see people using food as a means of reward or punishment: 'If I get through this I'm having a treat' or 'If you don't eat your veggies you can't have dessert'. Parents who use dessert as a bribe are teaching their children that veggies suck and sweets rock, a mindset that will help to create the next obese generation.

Having said that, I'm still a believer in counting calories, as it encourages us to think about the kinds of food we are eating. And yes, I'm aware that all calories are not created equal – that 100 calories from protein are not metabolised in the same way as 100 calories of carbohydrate (our bodies actually burn extra energy to break down protein) – but keeping an eye on your calorie quota means you are being mindful about what you're eating, and that's a good thing.

This is not a short-term weight-loss plan where you follow an eating and exercise regime for a few weeks so that you can fit into a wedding dress, but a life-long guide to nourishment. *Food for Life* has everything you need to get organised in the kitchen so that you take control of your health. I show you which foods to buy and why; I give you tips on shopping, preparing and storing food to save you time and money, and of course I've included 200 gorgeous wholefood recipes that tick all the boxes for high nutrition, lower calories and easy preparation. Plus you won't have to go to fancy shops to get the ingredients. I've also included helpful meal plans and shopping lists, as well as lots of ideas for lunchboxes, smoothies and snacks – even healthy pasta sauces, burgers and pizza.

This book is about getting back to basics in the kitchen and inspiring you to try new things. More than this, it's about enjoying nutritious food with people you love for the rest of your long, happy and healthy life.

'HERBS from my garden'

'FAMILY for LIFE'

PART ONE

EATING *for* LIFE

WHAT IS REAL FOOD?

Most of us think we understand which foods are 'good' for us – which foods are healthy – but do we *really*? I see people chugging back litres of 'zero-calorie' soft drinks thinking they're doing the right thing, yet the artificial sweeteners are keeping their tastebuds primed to crave sweetness. Others are dutifully serving pastry-based meals (pizza, quiches, pies) with a side of lettuce and tomato in the belief that it is doing them good. And yes it *is* way better than a wheelbarrow-load of deep-fried takeaway crap, but processed food is still full of bad fats, sugar and salt – it has to be, because the manufacturers are afraid we won't buy it if it's not; plus it lasts longer.

The truth is, the healthiest foods are wholefoods – nutrient-dense foods that are as close to their natural state as possible. This is 'real food' that's been dug out of the ground or picked off a tree rather than zapped with heat and chemicals, mixed with crazy additives and sealed in plastic. All of my recipes use wholefood ingredients that are easy to shop for, and every dish is easy to prepare and low in calories, plus it tastes amazing.

Yet I'm a realist. I know that for some people, shopping for food, let alone cooking it, can be overwhelming. Over the years I've worked with many people who need months of hand-holding and tears before they feel confident enough to take control of their health. Guiding them from greasy chips to organic veggies is not something that happens overnight – it's a gradual process, and is one reason I created my range Delicious Nutritious. Each meal provides three serves of vegetables and also introduces people to new ingredients and flavours. It might sound like a contradiction for me to be working with super-markets to offer packaged meals, but they are stepping stones on the road to better nutrition. Getting people into their kitchens and tasting nutritious food is a great first step. There's also another reason I created Delicious Nutritious: it's for people like me who love healthy food but sometimes find that life gets in the way (they get home really late, or they don't have the right ingredients).

THE FACTS ABOUT CARBS, PROTEIN & FATS

Everyone has a right to know what's in the food they eat and to understand whether or not it contributes to their health and wellbeing. But some of the fast-food and processed-food manufacturers spend an awful lot of money trying to ensure we *don't* know what's in their food, let alone what it does to our bodies – another reason I steer clear of stuff that doesn't look like real food. In this section I give you the lowdown on carbs, protein and fats and how our bodies metabolise them. I try not to make it sound like high-school science, but if your eyelids droop, please hang in there. Once you get a handle on this stuff, I know you will be inspired to make better food choices.

CARBS

Some people think carbohydrates are only found in foods like bread, pasta and rice. But carbs are actually found in virtually every food we eat except meat (yep, milk has carbs, along with all veggies, fruit, grains, nuts and seeds). Carbs are the body's primary energy source and are sometimes divided into 'simple' and 'complex'.

Simple carbs (often just called sugars) include the monosaccharides glucose and fructose and the disaccharides sucrose, dextrose and lactose. These guys give us an instant energy hit, but while glucose can be used by every cell in the body, fructose (fruit sugar) can only be metabolised in the liver. And here's the weird thing: most of the fructose we ingest is immediately converted to triglycerides (fat). The reason? When our ancestors were hunting and gathering, they only occasionally found berries and other fruits. So, to make the best use of this rare energy source, they were able to eat their fill and store it immediately as fat. In other words, we didn't evolve a 'full' switch that told our bodies we'd had enough fructose. More on that later.

Complex carbs include the polysaccharides starch and cellulose, which are found in fruits and veggies (especially the skins), nuts, seeds, legumes, wholegrain cereal (oats and brown rice) and wholegrain flour. Note that I said *whole*grain. Refined or highly processed grains (e.g. white flour in bread, cake, bikkies, pasta and noodles) have had the outer husk and germ removed (the nutritious bits), which means the starches are more rapidly converted to glucose in the body. In other words, they behave more like sugar. If you're going to eat a serve of bread or pasta, make it wholemeal or, better still, replace it with a serve of quinoa (see page 31), cauliflower rice (see page 151) or zucchini noodles (see page 218).

If you're going to eat BREAD or PASTA, make it WHOLEMEAL, or better still, replace it with quinoa, cauliflower rice or zucchini noodles.

- The fructose in table sugar (sucrose) is immediately stored as fat.
- Refined flour (pasta, bread etc) and starch (potato) is just like a sugar hit.
- Less than 10 per cent of our daily calories should come from added sugar.
- If we want to lose weight, sugar has to go.

OTHER NAMES FOR SUGAR

CORN SYRUP

DEXTROSE

DISACCHARIDES

FRUCTOSE

GLUCOSE

GOLDEN SYRUP

HONEY

LACTOSE

GALACTOSE

MALT

MALTOSE

MANNITOL

MAPLE SYRUP

MOLASSES

MONOSACCHARIDES

SORBITOL

SUCROSE

XYLITOL

How sugar makes us fat

In the last few years, sugar has copped some bad press. For good reason. We are eating way too much of it, even compared to just 50 years ago, and it's one of the reasons we have such high rates of obesity (62 per cent of us are overweight; 26 per cent are obese) along with the diseases that accompany it (such as fatty liver disease, diabetes and heart disease).

Every time we eat, the presence of glucose, amino acids or fatty acids in the intestine stimulates the pancreas to secrete a hormone called insulin. Its main job is to find all the excess glucose surging through our bloodstream and store it as glycogen in our liver and muscles. This is important, because too much glucose can lead to kidney damage, blindness and even amputation. But our bodies can only store enough glycogen for one active day. So, once we have filled up our stores, any extra floating around is converted to fat. Once the glucose is safely stored, our insulin levels drop back to normal again. This process is repeated every time we eat. If we eat a lot of sugar in one hit, we have an insulin spike, where our pancreas releases a stack of insulin to tell us we're full and to mop up all the glucose. When the insulin finishes its job, usually 1½–2 hours after eating, we get a sudden drop in glucose, which in turn triggers our hunger hormones (and also makes us feel flat and lacking in energy). So even though we don't *need* to eat any more food, our body is craving it.

The thing is, we're not just craving any food – we're craving sweet foods. Studies at NYU Langone Medical Center in 2015 found that insulin plays a much stronger role than previously thought in regulating the release of dopamine, a neurotransmitter that helps control the brain's reward and pleasure centres. This is how sugar can hook into our brain's reward pathways, so that we literally become addicted to the stuff.

How much sugar do we need?

When we're not eating anything, the amount of sugar in our bloodstream is about 1 teaspoon. In 2015, the World Health Organization recommended that free sugars ('monosaccharides and disaccharides added to foods and beverages by the manufacturer, cook or consumer, and sugars naturally present in honey, syrups, fruit juices and fruit juice concentrates') should comprise less than 10 per cent of our total energy intake. If you're eating 1600–1800 calories per day, the total amount of extra sugar in your diet should be around 8–9 teaspoons per day (using a 5-gram measure). Yet a 2012 report commissioned by the sugar industry found that the average adult consumption of sugar in Australia is around 27 teaspoons per day, and this figure doesn't even include honey, glucose, dextrose and syrups other than sucrose! A can of soft drink, for example, contains 33 grams of sugar, which is 7 teaspoons of sugar. That's close to your daily quota right there, without counting the sugar in your bread, jam, mayo . . .

How fibre and resistant starch keeps our gut bugs happy

There's another compelling reason why we should be amping up our intake of complex carbs: the fibre and resistant starches feed our gut bacteria. Now this might sound gross, but our gut contains a complicated ecosystem of bacteria (the 'microbiome') – trillions of tiny microbes that digest our food, provide many vitamins and nutrients and keep us healthy. (To give you an idea of size, you could fit a couple of million on the head of a pin.) Until recently we thought they were the bad guys, but the harmful ones (like salmonella) are a tiny minority and most play an essential role not only in the health of our digestive system, but also our immune system and even our moods.

It took millions of years to evolve this symbiotic relationship with our gut bacteria, where we provide them with a place to live and nutrients to grow in return for their help in breaking down food and keeping pathogenic bacteria in check. And we are only just beginning to understand how diet, medications like antibiotics, and our obsession with cleanliness have caused imbalances in the microbiome that could be linked with all sorts diseases from obesity and diabetes to asthma and eczema.

Ninety per cent of the SEROTONIN in our bodies is made in the GUT.

The walls of our intestines actually contain a network of neurons that communicate with our brains via the gut–brain axis. In fact, 90 per cent of the serotonin in our bodies is made in the gut. (Serotonin is a neurotransmitter that helps regulate mood, appetite, sleep, body temperature, memory and learning. In the gut it is used to control movement in the intestines, bowel and bladder. This is why people who have anxiety and depression often have digestive issues.) Recent studies have found that many gut bacteria can manufacture special proteins (peptides) that are very similar to hunger-regulating hormones, which means that they may be able to influence our eating behaviour.

Research in this area is still very new, but one thing scientists do agree on is that the more diverse our gut microbiome, the better our chances of staying healthy. Having fewer gut bug species is a common feature of obesity, inflammatory bowel disease and other conditions. Plus, there's evidence that a diverse microbiome can better resist invasive species like Salmonella. And what's the best way to encourage diversity? You guessed it – by eating as many different kinds of veggies, fruit, legumes and wholegrains as you can, along with yoghurt and lacto-fermented foods (try my Fermented Slaw on page 332).

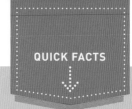

QUICK FACTS

▶ We have trillions of bacteria (our microbiome), most of them living in our colon.

▶ Our gut bugs break down fibre, fight off harmful bacteria and keep our colon healthy.

▶ We are healthier if we have lots of different species. A diet rich in fruit, veggies, wholegrains, nuts and seeds supports a diverse microbiome.

RESISTANT STARCH

Starch is a type of sugar found in most green plants (it's what plants use for energy), but unlike simple sugar, starch is a complex carbohydrate, which means it takes longer for our bodies to break it down. Resistant starches literally 'resist' being digested in the small intestine and instead pass straight into our colons where they feed the good bacteria that keep us healthy. Foods high in resistant starches include legumes, cashews, wholegrains and unripe bananas. Another source is starchy foods that have been cooked and then cooled, such as potato, pasta and rice – but they've got to be cold, otherwise they get digested before they reach the colon.

PROTEIN

Protein is essential for the building and repair of all of our body tissues and is found in meat, poultry, fish, dairy, beans, seeds and nuts. I want to explain a bit more about proteins so that you can understand why it's safe to crank up your veggie intake and dial down your animal protein.

Proteins are made up of chains of amino acids. There are 22 amino acids, nine of which we have to get from our diet because our bodies can't 'make' them. A protein source is considered 'complete' if it contains enough of each of the essential amino acids for us to stay healthy.

Generally, all of the proteins from animal foods (meat, fish, poultry, milk, eggs) are complete. Some of the proteins in plant foods (nuts, beans, seeds, grains and vegetables) can be complete, though there's usually not enough of each amino acid for optimum health. More often, plant proteins are missing one or more of the essential amino acids. Vegetarians and vegans know this; that's why they combine legumes with grains to create meals that are high in all of the essential amino acids. And if you think about it, this combination features in many traditional vegetarian dishes from all over the world, such as Mexican beans and corn, Japanese soybeans and rice, Cajun red beans and rice, and Indian dhal (lentils) and rice.

FATS

Fats are an important energy source and are necessary for healthy cell function, the absorption of certain vitamins (A, D, E and K), for maintaining body temperature and for healthy skin, hair and nails. Depending on their chemical composition, fats (fatty acids) are described as 'saturated', 'monounsaturated' and 'polyunsaturated', and most foods contain a combination of these.

Foods high in saturated fats include animal fats, whole-milk dairy products (milk, butter, cheese, yoghurt), coconut oil and palm kernel oil. Foods high in monounsaturated fats include olive oil, avocado, eggs, almonds, cashews and macadamias, while those high in polyunsaturated fats include seeds and seed oils (sunflower, safflower, linseed, sesame), legume oils (soybean and peanut), fish and walnuts.

Saturated v polyunsaturated

I've always said that when it comes to losing a lot of weight, reducing fat intake is crucial. This is because whether you're talking beef tallow or olive oil, all fats provide the same number of calories (9 calories per gram, compared with 4 calories per gram for protein and carbs), so if we eat more than we burn off, we're going to put on weight. And the more excess weight we carry, the greater our chances of developing cardiovascular disease and diabetes. But when it comes to the *types* of fats we should be eating, the story gets way more complicated.

For decades we've been told that saturated fats are evil, mostly because they are more readily stored as body fat and less easily used as fuel, and we've been advised to replace them with polyunsaturated ones. But while it's true that eating too much saturated fat is correlated with obesity and heart disease, recent research is finding that eating too much polyunsaturated oil may be just as bad, if not worse.

There are two polyunsaturated fatty acids that we have to get from our diet (our bodies can't make them): omega-3 and omega-6. These are important for normal growth and development, and for healthy brain function (our brains are actually 60 per cent fat!). Yet the amount we need is very small – about half a teaspoon of each per day. Also, the balance is crucial. If we get *way* more omega-6 than omega-3 (and some researchers estimate that we're eating more than twenty times as much omega-6) it will interfere with the absorption of omega-3, an imbalance that some believe to be a contributing factor in the rise of cardiovascular disease, autoimmune diseases like arthritis, inflammatory disease and even cancer.

There are several different types of omega-3 polyunsaturated fatty acids, but the long-chain omega-3s have been shown to have the most health benefits, particularly docosahexaenoic acid (DHA) and eicosapentaenoic acid (EPA), which are found in cold-water fish such as salmon, mackerel, sardines, tuna and herring.

Alpha-linolenic acid (ALA) is a plant-sourced short-chain omega-3 that's found in linseeds (also known as flaxseed), chia seeds, pumpkin seeds, canola, tofu and walnuts. However, ALA must be converted by the body to DHA and EPA, and because this synthesis is very inefficient we have to eat a lot more to get the same benefits as DHA and EPA.

But before you race out and buy 500 tins of tuna or a bucket of fish oil capsules, remember that you only need a tiny amount of omega-3. The best way to ensure you are getting enough omega-3 is to *reduce your intake of omega-6*. This means avoiding polyunsaturated oils that are high in omega-6, such as sunflower oil, grape seed oil, safflower oil, rice bran oil and anything labelled 'vegetable oil'. Canola oil, walnut oil and soybean oil contain some short-chain omega-3s (ALA), but they've still got a lot more omega-6, which probably cancels out any benefit you'd get from the ALA – you're better off with a sprinkle of pumpkin or chia seeds so you get the extra nutrients and fibre.

When it comes to oils, cold-pressed extra-virgin olive oil wins the healthy choice award. There are no chemicals or heat used in extraction and it's very low in both polyunsaturated omega-6 and saturated fat (it's mostly monounsaturated). Macadamia nut oil has a similar nutrient profile and is lovely in salads. I also don't mind using small amounts of coconut oil in cooking, as it's very stable at high temperatures. The same goes for butter though, like all fats, it's important to keep an eye on your portions.

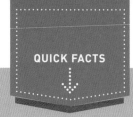

QUICK FACTS

- Use olive oil, macadamia nut oil, butter and coconut oil in moderation.

- Avoid vegetable oil, sunflower oil, safflower oil, peanut oil and rice bran oil.

- *Never* eat anything containing trans-fats.

OTHER NAMES FOR FAT

TALLOW

BUTTER

SHORTENING

COCONUT OIL

PALM OIL, PALM KERNEL OIL

COPHA

DRIPPING

LARD

VEGETABLE OILS AND FATS

HYDROGENATED OILS

GLYCEROL

PALM OIL (the oil from the fruit pulp and kernel of the oil palm) is the most widely produced edible oil in the world. It has a longer shelf life than other vegetable oils, making it more appealing for food production. It's found in about half of all the packaged foods on Australian shelves, including biscuits, chips, crackers, chocolate bars, brekkie cereals, two-minute noodles, packaged sweets, muesli bars, margarine and even sauces, curry paste and batters. It's also found in toothpaste, soap, washing powder, shampoo, moisturisers and cosmetics.

The problem is that the worldwide demand for this oil has led countries such as Indonesia and Malaysia to clear huge tracts of native forest to set up palm oil plantations. In fact, these two regions account for 85 per cent of global production of palm oil.

Palm oil plantations are now the leading cause of rainforest destruction in Malaysia and Indonesia, and this is destroying the habitat of some incredible wildlife, including the orang-utan. So vote with your dollar: don't buy products that contain palm oil, or better still, find companies that use sustainably sourced palm oil in their products. Organisations like the Worldwide Fund for Nature and the Orangutan Foundation should be able to help you find a list of these companies.

What's the deal with cholesterol?

We need cholesterol – it's an important building block for cell membranes, the hormones oestrogen and testosterone, vitamin D, and the bile acids that help us to digest fat. About 80 per cent of the body's cholesterol is produced by the liver, while the rest comes from our diet (mainly red meat, poultry, fish, eggs and dairy products).

Cholesterol is carried in the bloodstream by two kinds of lipoproteins: low-density lipoproteins (LDL) and high density lipoproteins (HDL). The low-density ones carry the cholesterol *from* the liver to the rest of the body, while the high-density ones carry excess cholesterol *back* to the liver for removal.

LDL cholesterol is called the 'bad' cholesterol because it is deposited along the inside of artery walls. Over time, this builds up to form a thick plaque that narrows the arteries (a process called atherosclerosis) and decreases blood flow through the narrowed area. Atherosclerosis is a precursor to coronary heart disease, stroke and peripheral artery disease.

Luckily, the HDL ('good') cholesterol is the one that's been extracted from the artery walls and is on its way back to the liver for disposal. So if you have more good cholesterol than bad, it will help protect you against heart disease and stroke.

Trans-fats

Trans-fats are used to increase the shelf life of processed foods like pies, pastries, cakes and biscuits. In a process called hydrogenation, liquid plant oils are made into solid ones by the addition of hydrogen atoms. (The name comes from the Latin word trans, which means 'across', because the hydrogen atoms in the double bond are actually across from each other.) Trans-fats are truly the kings of crap since they not only increase LDL (the bad) cholesterol, but also lower HDL (the good) cholesterol.

TRANS-FATS are truly the kings of CRAP.

However, trans-fats are only created when oils are *partially* hydrogenised. Fully hydrogenised oils don't have the same effect on cholesterol, so looking for the word 'hydrogenised' on a food label is not going to help you find out if it has trans-fats. Countries in Europe (Denmark, Norway, Iceland, Switzerland and Austria) have strict limits on the quantities of trans-fats in foods. But in Australia, manufacturers are not required to list trans-fats in the nutrition information panel unless there is a nutrition claim about other fats (such as omega-3, cholesterol or monounsaturated fat). All in all, another reason to run a mile from processed foods.

WHY I *Love* ETHICALLY PRODUCED FOOD

As the cost of living in our beautiful country escalates, it can be tempting to base our food choices on price only, especially when we're feeding a family. And when it comes right down to it, I'd rather my clients buy any kind of fresh veggies and meat, organic or not, than take a trip to the greasy drive-through. Yet as more and more people take on board the sustainability message, we are seeing a lot more ethically produced food. Personally, I love buying locally produced, certified-organic food because it not only tastes amazing, but also makes me feel good. I get a deep sense of satisfaction knowing that I am not only looking after my body, but also looking after the planet.

Ethically produced foods are those that have been grown, processed, distributed and used in a way that respects the people who make them, the people who eat them, the environment, and the foods themselves. So for farmers, ethical means having fair working conditions and getting paid properly; for food industry workers it means a healthy and safe workplace; for consumers it means the food is affordable and nutritious; for the environment it means the farming/production protects the planet and is sustainable; and finally, for the food itself, it means that animals are farmed without cruelty and crops are farmed with respect to their adaptability.

'Sustainable food' is a bit like a sub-category of ethical food. It takes into consideration the carbon footprint of harvesting, processing and packaging food, storing it in refrigerated containers and shipping it long distances. That adds up to many tonnes of CO_2 that could be avoided if we bought food grown locally. It also takes into account the future supply of the food itself. Sustainability in the fishing industry is a major issue given the depletion of species from over-fishing and heavy by-catch (i.e. all the other fish and sea creatures that die in the process of net fishing and trawling). I avoid buying threatened species by checking out the free app from the Australian Marine Conservation Society: Sustainable Seafood Guide.

I also try to buy food that is organic or biodynamic. Organic and biodynamic farming practices are similar in that they both exclude artificial chemicals and genetically modified materials, but biodynamic certification guidelines are much stricter. Biodynamic farms use preparations made from minerals and herbs to improve nutrient levels. Unfortunately, the word 'organic' is not regulated in Australia, so its use on a label doesn't guarantee that the product is genuinely free of pesticides, herbicides or hormones. To be certain you are buying genuinely organic or biodynamic produce, you need to look for a certification label. There are currently seven recognised certification bodies accredited and audited by the Australian Quarantine Inspection Service. Some smaller producers (especially at farmers' markets) actually do follow organic principles but can't afford certification – so always ask questions if you're unsure.

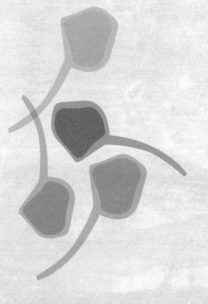

Vegetables

Vegetables are jam-packed with carbs for energy, fibre for digestive health and all the vitamins and minerals you need to properly metab-olise the proteins and other nutrients in your food. Eat them cooked or raw and in as many different colours as possible – especially the leafy green ones. Fresh is best, but don't be afraid to use frozen ones (their nutrient content is the same) or tinned ones occasionally – just be wary of additives and sugar, and always look for tins free from BPA plastic.

Because vegetables are so low in calories they are pretty much open slather when it comes to your daily intake. And even though some are higher in calories than others (e.g. sweet potato, avocado, sweetcorn), it's far better to be eating these than processed foods. You'll notice that all of my recipes feature vegetables and that the proportion of veggies is always larger than the meat.

YOUR VEGGIES DON'T NEED TO BE PERFECT

The big chains waste unbelievable amounts of fruit and veg, rejecting 20–40 per cent of produce grown by suppliers because it is not the right shape or colour. Look for a supermarket that sells imperfect fruit and veg. It's up to us to buy the wonky ones – after all, they taste exactly the same.

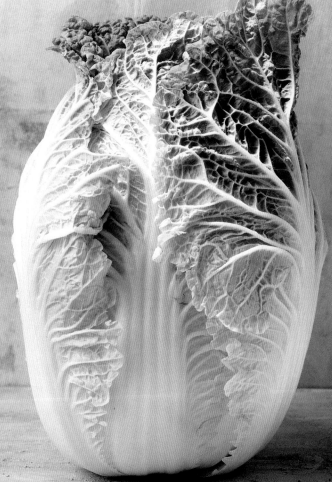

VEGGIES are the ROCK-STAR ATTRACTION . . . the meat is just the back-up singer.

Here is a list of VEGGIES that I LOVE to use in my cooking.

Asparagus: I can't wait for spring and summer when asparagus is at its best. I love its amazing flavour, shape and colour. It's also a good source of fibre and folate. Snap off the woody ends and store the spears in a glass of water in your fridge door if you can't use them immediately.

Avocado: Avocadoes contain about 10–15 per cent fat, most of which is monounsaturated (like olive oil). Keep the stone in the avocado after cutting, and sprinkle the cut part with lemon juice to reduce oxidation.

Beetroot: Comes from the same family as silverbeet and spinach – no wonder it's so full of vitamins and minerals. Plus I adore the rich, purple-red colour. Grate it raw in salads, or scrub it, chop into chunks and roast with a little oil. Add the leaves to a mixed leaf salad – they're a good source of iron.

Bok choy: This popular Asian green is from the cabbage family and has white stems and dark green leaves; it's delicious in stir-fries, or steamed as a side. The smaller variety (baby bok choy) is lighter in colour and has a milder flavour.

Broccoli: Brimming with vitamins A, C and K plus potassium, magnesium and plenty of fibre, this super veggie also contains a sulfur compound called sulforaphane, which is strongly associated with a reduced risk of cancer. Broccoli is great in soups, stews, stir-fries or simply baked or steamed and sprinkled with sesame seeds. Most people eat the florets, but the stem is sweet and full of nutrients.

Broccolini: Some people think this is baby broccoli, but it's actually a hybrid of broccoli and gai lan. It's tender and sweet and I love that you can eat the stems, too.

Brussels sprouts: These 'mini cabbages' are right up there with broccoli for nutrient content. Slice them, brush them with olive oil or coconut oil and pop them on the barbie – delicious.

Cabbage: Red cabbage is a bit sweeter and has six times as much vitamin C as white or green cabbage. Slice cabbage finely to make a crunchy salad base, or try making Fermented Slaw (see page 332).

Capsicum: Red, yellow and orange varieties are sweeter than the green ones, but they've all got a fair whack of vitamin C. Roast them to remove the skins if you like and store them in the fridge to add to wraps, salads and pizza.

Carrots: A great source of fibre and beta-carotene, which is converted in the body to vitamin A. Carrots were originally purple, and you can now buy the purple heirloom varieties in most supermarkets.

Cauliflower: Like its cousins cabbage and broccoli, cauli is a cruciferous veggie with plenty of vitamin C, fibre and other nutrients. I love making cauli mash, but you can also chop it finely and use it instead of rice (see page 151). (Lightly steam or saute your cauli rice unless you don't mind farting like a train!)

Celeriac: This knobbly veggie is, you guessed it, related to celery and has a similar flavour though a bit earthier/nuttier. Use it in soups, stews and mash or grate it with other veggies to make fritters.

Celery: Don't forget to use the leaves in soups or stir-fries; the inner leaves are delicious in salads.

Choy sum: Another nutritious cruciferous veggie, this one has green stems, longish, flat leaves and sometimes little yellow flowers.

Cucumber: A crisp, fresh addition to any salad, Lebanese and continental cucumbers have smaller seeds than the large, bumpy standard ones.

Eggplant: Sometimes called aubergines, the bell-shaped purple ones are the most common, though you can also get long, thin ones, and different-coloured ones. Eggplant is an excellent source of vitamin B6, and the skin is high in antioxidants.

Fennel: This is actually a flowering plant in the carrot family. The white bulb has a delicate sweet flavour – slice it finely in a salad or add it to soups, stir-fries and slow-cooked dishes. The fronds (and seeds) are edible, too, and have a flavour similar to aniseed.

Gai lan: Also called Chinese broccoli, this Asian veggie looks more like light-green silverbeet than broccoli, but with chunky green stems.

Gai choy: This green leafy veggie has thick, ribbed stems, crinkly leaves and a strong, peppery flavour – which is why it's also called Chinese mustard.

Kale: Another nutrient-rich relative of cabbage and broccoli, you can get curly leaf varieties and the darker, thin-leafed ones (Tuscan kale or cavolo nero). Loaded with vitamins A and C, kale is great for detoxing and also has anti-inflammatory benefits. I love tossing a few leaves on the barbie when I'm searing some fresh salmon.

Lettuce: There's iceberg (crisp head), mignonette (butter head) and cos (romaine), though cos has more fibre and vitamins A and C than the other varieties. I love to fill an iceberg or cos leaf with a little tuna and salad for the healthiest wrap on the planet.

Mushrooms: The common mushroom has different names depending on when it's harvested. Button mushrooms are the baby ones (champignons), caps or swiss browns are a bit bigger, and then flats, field mushrooms or portobellos are the biggest ones. You can also get exotics such as oyster and shiitake. Mushrooms contain most of the B group vitamins, especially riboflavin (B2), niacin (B3), pantothenic acid and biotin, though unlike most vegetables, they have little vitamin A or C. They're also a good source of dietary fibre, potassium, zinc and selenium.

Onions: There are many varieties of onion, including brown, white, red, spring onions (also called green onions) and shallots. Red onions are great for salads because they're milder and sweeter.

Pak choy: This is often confused with bok choy, but is smaller, and has greenish, spoon-shaped stems (not white). It also has a milder and sweeter flavour.

Parsnips: Another delicious, sweet-tasting root vegetable. Lovely baked as it is, or added to soups. Slice it into rounds and make crispy parsnip chips, or grate it and add to fritters.

Potatoes: I've always steered clear of white potatoes, but if you leave the skins on, the ones with creamy, waxy flesh (such as kipfler or desiree) have a delicious flavour and texture. Also, if you eat them cold, you'll reduce their glycaemic load and create resistant starches (see page 10).

Pumpkin: Bell-shaped butternuts are the sweetest, then there's the small golden nugget, the big Queensland blues (which are actually grey) and the Kent or Jap (short for 'Just a Pumpkin') have speckled, grey-green skin.

Rocket: This salad green is another cruciferous vegetable with a strong, peppery flavour. It makes a great addition to a salad mix.

Silverbeet: Sometimes called swiss chard, this super-nutritious green has an earthy flavour and is a good source of folate, fibre, magnesium and vitamins A and C. Chop it finely and add it to salads, soups or stews. Or use it as a replacement when any recipe calls for spinach.

Spinach: This one may just take the crown when it comes to vegetable royalty. Some people confuse it with silverbeet, but spinach has smaller, light-green leaves, slender stalks and a much milder flavour. It's a great source of iron, vitamin C, folate and magnesium. You can pretty much sneak baby spinach into any meal: add a handful to soups or smoothies, or sprinkle it over a just-cooked pizza or omelette and let it wilt deliciously.

Squash: A relative of pumpkin, melon and zucchini, the lovely yellow colour and unusual shape of these little veggies make them a great side dish.

Swede: Believe it or not, swedes are another member of the huge cabbage family. They have a similar texture to turnips, but are a lot sweeter. Add them to stews or winter soups.

Sweet potatoes: I use this amazing tropical veggie as an alternative to potatoes because of its high nutrient content, specifically beta-carotene and vitamins C and E. Weirdly, it's not even related to the spud, but to morning glory vine. Australia grows the gold (orange), red, purple and white varieties. Scrub them, no need to peel them – they make delicious mash and chips, or just slice them up, brush them with olive oil and roast them on the barbie.

Tomatoes: These are available in so many varieties, colours and sizes that it can be hard to choose. Truss tomatoes taste the best, though homegrown cherry tomatoes are unbeatable. They're all a great source of vitamin C (cherry tomatoes have the most) and supply some vitamin E, folate and fibre.

Turnips: These old-fashioned veg have a strong flavour – younger, smaller ones are sweeter and milder. Add to soups and stews, and use their leafy tops like spinach.

Watercress: This little aquatic plant was recently named the most nutrient-dense fruit/veggie on the planet. It contains a huge amount of vitamins A and C, plus a bunch of other vitamins.

Wombok (Chinese cabbage): Like watercress, one of the most nutrient-dense veggies around. I use it in stir-fries and salads.

Zucchini: These are an excellent source of vitamin C, fibre and other nutrients and are really versatile. Grate in salads, omelettes and wraps; add to pasta sauces, stews and soups; or, best of all, slice into long strips to make zucchini noodles (see page 218).

KALE is great for DETOXING and also has ANTI-INFLAMMATORY BENEFITS.

I love tossing a few leaves on the BARBIE
when I'm searing some fresh SALMON.

WATERCRESS, SPINACH, KALE and ROCKET are all good sources of IRON, essential for red blood cell formation.

WATERCRESS and WOMBOK (CHINESE CABBAGE) are the most nutrient-dense veggies you can eat.

I eat BROCCOLI and SPINACH pretty much EVERY DAY.

PARSLEY is high on the list of NUTRIENT-DENSE veggies.

RADISH and
PARSLEY are
surprisingly
rich sources of
VITAMIN C.

CARROT, SWEET POTATO, PUMPKIN
and CAPSICUM are full of VITAMIN A,
which maintains EYE HEALTH, as well
as a healthy REPRODUCTIVE SYSTEM.

CAULI makes GREAT MASH.

I love BARBECUING SWEET POTATO.

BRUSSELS, CAULI and CAPSICUM contain FOLATE,
essential for pregnant women as it plays
a crucial role in the formation of a developing
child's brain and spinal cord.

ROOT VEGGIES
are high in FIBRE.

WHAT IS REAL FOOD?

Fruit

Fruits are higher in calories (and fructose) than vegetables so it's best to eat them in moderation – no more than two pieces a day. Strawberries and blueberries are low in sugar compared with other fruits, but that doesn't mean you should scoff the whole punnet. Also note that the riper a fruit, the more sugar it contains.

Dried fruits are a good way to sweeten food, but they are naturally high in fructose and glucose, so keep them to a minimum. Also, try to source ones that are dried naturally without preservatives – some people react badly to sulphur dioxide. If you want to eat a couple of dates as a snack, make sure you have them with a few nuts to lower their glycaemic index and avoid an insulin spike.

Frozen berries are fine (they've often been grown with fewer pesticides), though the ones in supermarket chains are often shipped from China or Mexico; check the packaging. And please, forget tinned fruit – it is swimming in sugar, it doesn't tick any nutritional boxes, and the plastic lining in the tins can be a source of BPA (bisphenol-A), a chemical that can mess with your hormones.

Please, FORGET TINNED fruit – it's swimming in SUGAR.

FRUITS I LOVE

Here is a list of FRUITS I LOVE to eat and use in my cooking.

WHAT ABOUT ANTIOXIDANTS?

Our bodies need oxygen to break down food, but this process naturally creates 'free radicals' – atoms or molecules with unpaired electrons. These rush around looking to steal an electron from other molecules and substances, messing with their structure and function. Luckily, we have developed natural defences against them – antioxidants, which are able to donate electrons without turning into free radicals themselves. While we know that free radicals contribute to illnesses like heart disease, cancer and Alzheimer's, this doesn't necessarily mean that taking antioxidant supplements will prevent disease. In fact, aside from one study showing they may help prevent age-related macular degeneration, the rest don't support it at all. If we focus on eating a healthy diet, we'll be getting enough antioxidants to keep the natural free radicals in check. The bottom line? Keep it as real as possible.

Apples: Depending on the variety, they're available year-round. Don't peel your apples; the skin is where a lot of the nutrients hang out.

Blueberries: Low in sugar, gorgeous colour, subtle flavour and grown year-round here in Australia. I love to add a few to smoothies and muffins.

Goji berries: Their sweet and sour taste makes them a great addition to smoothies, homemade muesli and porridge. They're a good source of iron, vitamin C and the antioxidant lycopene (the carotenoid that gives them their colour).

Grapes: The seedless varieties are my favourites. Add them to salads, or freeze them to make a great summer snack for the kids.

Honeydew melon: This melon has pale-green flesh and a more subtle flavour than rockmelon.

Kiwi fruit: I'm a big fan of this super fruit. It's high in vitamin C (much higher than citrus) and fibre (especially if you scrub the skin instead of peeling).

Lemons & limes: These zingy fruits are a key ingredient in dressings and many Asian and Indian dishes. I love adding a pinch of lemon zest to lamb.

Mangoes: This sweet tropical fruit brings back childhood memories of sitting out in the backyard, happily slopping juice everywhere! Nowadays I know how to halve them, and cross-hatch each half so I can eat inside!

Oranges: They not only contain vitamin C, but beta-carotene and other flavonoids that have an antioxidant effect in the body. They are also high in pectin, a type of fibre that helps keep your intestines healthy. Add grated zest to cereal for extra zing and goodness.

Pomegranate: The seeds look gorgeous in salads. To remove them, carefully score the pomegranate around the middle, hold it over a bowl and break it in half. Now squeeze each half to loosen the seeds, tapping them out on the side of the bowl. Freeze them when pomegranates are in season or use goji berries instead.

Raspberries: These divine little berries are actually related to roses. They've got a heap of vitamin C and fibre. I could quite happily eat a handful of raspberries in place of dessert and never feel like I'm missing out.

Rockmelon: Also called cantaloupe, this sweet-tasting melon is high in vitamin C, beta-carotene and potassium. It tastes best in summer, though you can get it year-round.

Strawberries: One of my favourite fruits, and so versatile. My nanna grew them in her garden in Barraba and I loved going out to pick them with her.

Seafood, Poultry & Red Meat

We are very lucky in Australia to be able to choose from an amazing variety of protein sources that don't cost an arm and a leg. But many of us get into the habit of using the same ones over and over, often because they feature in a handful of recipes we're comfortable with and it seems easier to stick with what we know. Here are some of the animal proteins I love to use.

Seafood

Seafood has always been a winner for me. It's generally only around 1 calorie per gram and is so nutritious. It's got protein, selenium, zinc and iodine; some species also have vitamins A and D. Fish is an excellent source of DHA and EPA, the long-chain omega-3 fatty acids that are well known for their health benefits. Research has shown that eating fish regularly – two or three serves weekly – may reduce the risk and/or severity of cardiovascular disease, though only if you're already eating a good balance of macronutrients. (It's not going to work to have salmon a couple of times a week if for the rest of the time you're eating burgers, fries or drinking boxes of wine.)

There are so many different ways to prepare seafood – barbecued, baked, poached, grilled, steamed. I never eat battered fish because the flour and oil double the calories. Plus, unless I cook it myself, I can't be sure what kind of oil is used, or what's in the batter, which breaks one of my golden rules – always know exactly what you're eating.

Salmon is a particular favourite. Besides that lovely silken texture, gorgeous colour and rich flavour, I always feel that I can virtually taste the goodness of all the omega-3 and vitamin D. When I eat it fresh, I try to buy wild-caught Eastern Australian salmon or Western Australian salmon (also called bay trout, cocky salmon, colonial salmon, salmon trout and New Zealand kahawai). Australian farmed Atlantic salmon is the next option – it's farmed in Tassie and is way preferable to buying fish from overseas (check the packaging). For convenience, I sometimes use tins of salmon or tuna, though I always check the label to make sure it's sustainably caught. Look for 'pole-and-line-caught' on the label. However, it's important to remember that larger fish like shark, Atlantic salmon and tuna tend to have high mercury levels, so it's good to also eat smaller fish like sardines, whiting and mackerel.

Poultry

Chicken is another of my staple protein sources and I've always been passionate about ethically raised birds. Unlike factory-farmed chooks, free-range chickens are allowed to run around outside during the day and aren't given antibiotics. However, only certified organic chickens have been fed organic pellets. The Sustainable Table website has lots more information.

Red meat

Kangaroo is at the top of my list of lean meats. It's high in protein, low in fat (less than 2 per cent) and high in omega-3, which assists in lowering cholesterol. It's super-low in calories as well – even lower than a lot of fish! It's also organic (no hormones or chemicals) and is more environmentally friendly than other sources of red meat, as kangaroos produce no methane gas and, being soft-footed, create no soil degradation. Virtually drought proof and requiring far less food than cattle, they spend their entire lives in their natural habitat, and are humanely culled by experts. You will find some fabulous recipes for kangaroo in this book, and most of the beef recipes (except the beef stock) can be adapted for kangaroo.

When buying beef, I avoid grain-fed beef, because the meat is significantly lower in nutrients and tends to be higher in fat. Plus, grain-fed cattle are kept in feedlots whereas their grass-fed counterparts live on open pasture. I also try to source organic beef, and although it can be quite expensive I only use it occasionally and make sure the portions are small.

I rarely eat pork, due to its long history of unethical farming practices. However, the pork industry has changed a lot in the last 10 years. The Australian Pork Industry Quality Assurance system has three different accreditations: indoor, outdoor bed, and free-range. To qualify as free-range, the pigs have to be outside the whole time, have access to fresh bedding, shelter and a muddy wallow (that's how they cool down), and room to do what pigs love to do – rooting around in the dirt.

To ensure you are getting quality meat, it's a great idea to develop a good relationship with your local butcher – I always do. Talk to them about where they source their meat and ask them about the farming practices of the suppliers. If they don't know, find a butcher who does.

KANGAROO is at the TOP of my list of LEAN MEATS.

Eggs & Dairy Foods

Eggs and dairy foods are rich sources of protein from animals. Eating products from humanely raised chickens, cows, goats and sheep is much more sustainable than eating the animals themselves.

Eggs

When you look at all the nutrients that eggs contain inside those fragile shells, it can blow your mind: protein, omega-3 fats, zinc and several crucial vitamins. They are also a good source of the amino acid tryptophan, which the body uses to make serotonin, a neurotransmitter important in mood, memory processing, sleep and cognition. Go for organic, free-range varieties whenever possible – healthier hens produce more nutritious eggs.

Dairy foods

Dairy foods include milk, cheese and yoghurt – all of which are great sources of protein, calcium and energy. Some people prefer not to eat dairy products for various reasons: they might be vegan, lactose-intolerant or they might not enjoy the taste. But calcium is especially important for women. If we don't get enough in our diet we have a greater risk of developing osteoporosis (brittle bone disease) later in life.

Dietary guidelines recommend that adults need 2½ serves of dairy food a day (menopausal women need 4 serves):

1 serve
- ▶ 1 cup milk
- ▶ 1 cup soy, rice or nut milk, with at least 100 mg of added calcium per 100 ml
- ▶ 2 slices (40 g) hard cheese
- ▶ ½ cup fresh ricotta
- ▶ ¾ cup yoghurt

If you don't eat dairy at all, to get the same amount of calcium in 1 serve, you need to eat:
- ▶ 100 g almonds with skin on
- ▶ 60 g sardines
- ▶ 100 g tinned pink salmon with bones
- ▶ 100 g firm tofu (check the label as calcium levels vary)

LACTOSE INTOLERANCE

Lactose is the carbohydrate found in milk that gives it its naturally sweet taste. Our bodies need the enzyme lactase to break it down into glucose and galactose so we can use it for energy. Most people are born with the ability to produce the lactase enzyme because breast milk, like cow's milk, contains lactose. But some people are genetically predisposed to lose this ability as they grow older and they become lactose intolerant, causing cramps, bloating, gas and diarrhoea.

However, lactose intolerance is not black and white: sometimes your gut bacteria can handle lactose even if your DNA doesn't tell your body to make lactase. Research has shown that the majority of people with low lactase enzyme levels can still handle 1–2 cups of milk a day, especially if they're spread out over the day. Interestingly, cheese has two advantages over milk for the lactose intolerant — it's lower in lactose, and its higher fat content slows down absorption.

I've never been a big milk drinker; I much prefer yoghurt or cheese. However, as I explained earlier, 'low fat' dairy products aren't necessarily 'low calorie'. That's because the fat content is what makes them tasty, and once manufacturers take it out, they'll often replace it with sugar so people still like the taste. The bottom line with dairy is that you need to make a little go a long way. Some of the low-fat, low-calorie cheeses can have very little flavour and you can wind up eating more. I often have full-fat yoghurt or full-flavoured cheese that I can actually taste and enjoy, but only have a small portion. As always, it's about reading the label, knowing the calories and nailing your portion sizes.

The bottom line with DAIRY is that you need to make a LITTLE go a LONG WAY.

Yoghurt

It's widely accepted that the live cultures in yoghurt help to keep our digestive systems functioning well. And, being made from milk, yoghurt also contains a lot of calcium, which is excellent for our bones. But did you know that yoghurt is also good for your brain? It contains magnesium, which helps facilitate metabolic functions, particularly in the grey matter upstairs. However, go to any supermarket and you will be so dazzled by the yoghurt selection that it is almost impossible to choose. I'll tell you now that 90 per cent of them are sugar-filled rubbish. You want a plain yoghurt with no sugar or fruit added (it's usually a concentrate or conserve packed with sugar) that contains live cultures.

It can be easy to see yoghurt just as something to add to your breakfast cereal or as a quick snack – and it is perfect for both those things – but it is a much more versatile ingredient than that. I use it in soups, as a dressing for salads and an accompaniment to stews. I also use it to make my own labne, which is a super-healthy cream cheese (see page 333). By adding a little salt to some organic full-fat yoghurt, and straining it for 24 hours, you add heaps more good bacteria to the culture (lactobacilli thrive on salt).

Grains, Nuts, Seeds, Lentils & Beans

When it comes to fuelling our bodies, this food group is the engine room. The carbs in these foods are released nice and slowly, keeping us feeling fuller for longer. Plus they all contain vegetable proteins and give our gut bugs plenty to chew on.

Grains

Grains include wheat, rye, oats, barley, spelt and rice. The outside layer contains a lot of important nutrients, and in most grains it is rich in fibre. Refined white flour (used in most breads, biscuits, cereals etc) has had this outer layer removed, so is far less nutritious, and is virtually useless when it comes to keeping us 'regular'. Yet we are so used to filling up on these refined carbohydrates that many of us don't even realise the value of wholegrain alternatives.

BREAD Always buy wholegrain or wholemeal flatbread, loaves or rolls. I don't eat a lot of bread, and when I do it's always in the morning or for lunch, never at night (unless I'm having a special evening out and it's artisan bread made by the chef!). I like soy and linseed or a good-quality sourdough for breakfast or lunch. Genuine sourdough is made with a lacto-fermented culture, which means it's easier to digest.

RICE Rice is an excellent way of pumping up the calorie count of a stir-fry for growing kids or any manual workers in the household. For weight-loss candidates though, rice should be avoided. Brown rice has a lower GI than white, and long-grain rice a lower GI than short. I prefer doongara or basmati rice and usually eat it at lunch time rather than at night.

PASTA Pasta often gets a bum rap, even though it's an excellent source of energy. Wholegrain pasta has way more fibre and is higher in protein than ordinary durum wheat pasta and has a nuttier, chewier texture. However, like rice and bread, it's still a load of carbs so portion size is critical, as is what you serve it with and when. I try to reserve my pasta dishes for lunch, in small portions, and always follow them with a smashing training session later on. Like rice, pasta is something you can feed to children or to family members who do a lot of physical work, but if you want to stay lean, simply replace it with thinly sliced zucchini and carrot, or extra green veggies. Oh, and always serve your pasta 'al dente' – firm to the bite – to slow down digestion. If you overcook it, the starches are absorbed quickly. Another option is to serve it cold to amp up the resistant starch (see info on page 10).

GLUTEN

About 1 in 100 Australians have coeliac disease, where the immune system reacts abnormally to gluten, attacking the gut lining. This reduces nutrient absorption and causes a range of gastrointestinal and malabsorptive symptoms, including chronic diarrhoea, anaemia and muscle wasting. Gluten intolerance, on the other hand, is a reaction that doesn't involve the immune system. Symptoms include cramps, bloating, wind or diarrhoea. However, researchers have found some people who believe they are gluten-intolerant are actually reacting to the fermentation of other nutrients in their gut – FODMAPS (fermentable oligosaccharides, disaccharides, mono-saccharides and polyols). If you think you are gluten-intolerant, see your doctor *before* you go gluten-free (you need to be eating gluten for the test to work). Plus, a lot of the gluten-free food you see on supermarket shelves is full of sugar.

The carbs in WHOLEGRAINS are released nice and slowly, keeping us FULLER FOR LONGER.

NOODLES Noodles are most often associated with Asian cuisine and are made from a variety of starches that soak up the flavours of the soups or sauces they are served with. There are lots to choose from: rice noodles (thin like vermicelli, or wider and flat like fettuccine); bean noodles (made from mung bean starch); udon and ramen noodles (both contain some wheat); sweet potato noodles; and soba noodles (made with buckwheat flour, although many also contain wheat flour: check the ingredients). Forget instant noodles – they're usually high in salt and/or sugar and have a higher GI than their fresh counterparts.

WHAT IS REAL FOOD?

Nuts

Like seeds, nuts are nutritional powerhouses, containing carbs, good fats, amino acids, vitamins and lots of minerals. They also provide a heap of fibre, which is great for the digestive system. Studies suggest that nuts like walnuts, pistachios, almonds and pecans may lower serum LDL cholesterol and/or raise HDL (the good cholesterol), which is why many doctors advise people with high cholesterol to eat a handful of nuts a day.

Almonds: Almonds contain the most protein of all the tree nuts, plus lots of vitamin E. They seem to be everywhere at the moment: there's almond spread, almond milk and almond meal (flour) as well as raw almonds, roasted almonds and the slivered and blanched almonds you'll find in the baking aisle.

Cashews: Cashews are high in zinc, and have the lowest fat content of all the tree nuts. Cashew spread is available in most supermarkets.

Hazelnuts: These have a similar nutrient profile to macadamias. I've also used hazelnut spread in a couple of recipes; you can find it in health-food stores or online.

Macadamias: These have the highest fat content of all the tree nuts, and make an excellent monounsaturated oil.

Peanuts: Okay, I know these are legumes, but no one soaks and cooks them like kidney beans, so they stay here. Peanuts are the most common food allergen in Australia, followed by shellfish, fish, tree nuts and eggs.

Pecans: These are also high in omega-3, though walnuts have ten times as much!

Pine nuts: Pine nuts are the magic ingredient in basil pesto, and are delicious added to salads. Toast them gently over low heat in a dry pan to release their delicious flavour. (Be careful, though: they burn in a second if you're not paying attention.)

Pistachios: These actually contain the same amount of protein as almonds. Their lovely colour makes them a great garnish.

Walnuts: These guys have a huge whack of short-chain omega-3s (ALA), which is why I've used them in several recipes. Look for Australian-grown ones.

QUICK FACTS

COCONUT

Some people think coconuts are nuts, but they're actually 'drupes' – fruits that are fleshy on the outside and contain a hard shell with a seed on the inside. (Just to confuse you, lots of other so-called nuts are technically drupes too, including pecans, walnuts, almonds and pistachios.) Coconut has a good amount of iron and other minerals and stacks of fibre. You can get coconut flour, desiccated or shredded coconut, and coconut milk or cream, which is made by simmering coconut meat with water and straining the liquid (the 'cream' version just uses 75 per cent less water).

Seeds

Seeds contain fewer calories than nuts, but still give you that same satisfied feeling when you eat them. Poppy seeds, sesame seeds and linseeds are great for sprinkling over a dish after it has been cooked, and pumpkin seeds (pepitas) and sunflower seeds are great for snacking or to sprinkle over salads. Seeds like amaranth, buckwheat and quinoa (pronounced 'KIN-wah') are sometimes called ancient grains because they have more starch than most other small seeds, but they are not true grains. They don't come from grasses and are completely gluten-free – all three are the seeds of flowering, leafy plants.

Buckwheat: These seeds come from a plant in the rhubarb family, and are high in vitamin B6, potassium and magnesium, and also contain some iron. You can pre-soak, rinse and then cook them to serve as an alternative to rice (they have a stronger, nutty flavour). Or you can buy **buckinis** from health-food stores. These have been soaked and dried at a low temperature to preserve their nutrients. Buckinis can be used as a cereal and make a great base for tabbouleh.

Chia: A true super-seed, chia is high in short-chain omega-3 fatty acids, calcium, protein and fibre. You can get Australian-grown white or black chia. Add it to porridge, muesli, smoothies, homemade muffins, slices or puddings. I've included an easy recipe for Strawberry Chia Jam on page 89.

Quinoa: High in fibre and minerals, this ancient seed is a great replacement for rice. There are several varieties (white, black, red and purple), though so far only the white variety is grown in Australia. Don't to forget to rinse the quinoa *really* well before you cook it to remove the saponin (the coating that protects the seeds from insects and bug destruction). You can also buy quinoa flakes and puffed quinoa, which are good for making your own muesli.

Sesame seeds: If you eat these unprocessed (i.e. not as an oil or tahini) these little guys are super-high in calcium, iron, magnesium, vitamin B6 and fibre. You can get white and black varieties: sprinkle them over salads and cooked dishes, or add them to homemade snack bars.

Lentils & Beans

Legumes such as lentils, beans, soybeans and chickpeas have some unique advantages over other foods: they are cheap, they last just about forever and they are really versatile. Plus, they have a low carbon footprint (producing 1 kg of beef emits nine times more greenhouse gas than 1 kg of legumes and uses eighteen times as much water). They are packed with protein and low-GI carbohydrates along with cholesterol-lowering fibre, B group vitamins and folate. You'll find lots of recipes with beans and lentils in this book, like Mediterranean Beans (see page 104) and Fresh Four Bean Nachos (see page 222). Most recipes suggest using tinned beans for convenience, which is fine as long as you drain and rinse them.

Black beans: Also called turtle beans.

Borlotti beans: These are creamy coloured with red speckles; often used in Italian dishes.

Brown/green lentils: Dried lentils cook faster than dried beans, though organic tinned lentils are also readily available.

Butter beans: Also called lima beans, these are large and flat and have a really creamy texture.

Cannellini beans: White beans with a kidney-bean shape and a mild, creamy flavour.

Chickpeas: The larger kabuli chickpea is a Middle Eastern staple; there are also smaller desi chickpeas used in Indian cuisine.

Edamame: Soybeans, also available frozen in Asian groceries and some big supermarkets.

Navy beans: Also called haricot beans, these small white legumes are used to make commercial baked beans.

Puy lentils: Also called 'French-style lentils', these are smaller than brown or green lentils and hold their shape after cooking.

Red kidney beans: Their rich red colour make kidney beans a great addition to salads.

Red lentils: No need to buy these in tins; they cook up quickly and absorb all the juices in whatever you're cooking (e.g. soup, curry, stew).

Sprouts

Bean and seed sprouts are little nutritional powerhouses, containing protein, vitamins, minerals and fibre. If you've never tried sprouting before, it's really easy and fun for the kids. You don't need any expensive hoo-hah. Just some alfalfa seeds or mung beans in a jar, with a piece of fine-mesh cloth elastic-banded over the top (use a new Chux if you like). Now just rinse them once a day and leave them upside down to drain. Add the fresh sprouts to wraps, sandwiches and salads; they make a great garnish on soups and stews, too.

QUICK FACTS

PHYTIC ACID

Nuts, cereal grains, seeds and beans all contain phytic acid to protect them against attack from insects, and to stop them germinating at the wrong time. The problem is that when we ingest phytic acid, it reduces the absorption of minerals such as calcium, magnesium, iron and zinc. This is why it's important to soak dried beans before you cook them.

Fats & Oils

As we saw earlier (see page 11), advice about dietary fats can be quite confusing. I've always advised clients to reduce all the fats in their diet, whether they are saturated or not, and to ramp up their vegetables and protein. If we're eating minimally processed proteins and carbs, then we're already getting enough fats to keep us healthy. I think it's more important to focus on the kind of food we are eating, rather than the kind of fat it contains. For example, someone might not put butter on their toast (for fear of its saturated fat content), yet happily spread a couple of heaped tablespoons of marmalade on it instead (the high fructose is instantly stored as fat). Or they might not eat chips with their pub meal, yet drink half a bottle of wine (no explanation needed here).

Olive oil: I've always used olive oil. It's a monounsaturated fat, which means it's stable at moderate temperatures and doesn't go rancid (oxidise) like polyunsaturated oils do. I'll often use olive oil spray for cooking, as it helps me to control how much I use.

Butter: I don't eat margarine as it is processed from omega-6 oils using industrial chemicals. Butter is more than 80 per cent saturated fat, yet contains no emulsifiers, flavours or other crappy ingredients. However, just because you wouldn't grease your bike chain with margarine doesn't mean you can hoe down on butter. I use it sparingly.

Macadamia oil: Macadamia oil has a delicate flavour and is high in monounsaturated fats (though it has hardly any omega-3). It makes a lovely salad dressing.

Coconut oil: Many people avoid coconut oil because it is 90 per cent saturated fat. And I did too until I did my research and discovered that not all saturated fats are created equal. Coconut oil is made up of medium-chain triglycerides, which are more quickly metabolised than the long-chain triglycerides in animal fats. Some studies have shown that these make us feel fuller, and that they may also increase HDL cholesterol. However, like all fats, we need to keep an eye on how much we use as they contain double the calories found in carbs and protein. Coconut oil comes in jars and is usually solid at room temperature, though will start to melt above 21–25°C. It has a *really* long shelf life if you store it out of the sun and use a clean teaspoon to remove it from the jar. Coconut oil spray is also a good option for frying.

Herbs, Spices
& other flavour kicks

When life is hectic, and I don't have time to attempt a chef imperson-ation, I fire up the barbie, grab some fish or meat to grill, make a salad and that's dinner on the table in 20 minutes. Steve and I never get sick of it. The reason? We add delicious flavour bursts with these herbs and spices below.

Basil: One of my favourite herbs. Make batches of pesto and freeze so you can have it all year.

Cardamom: Cardamom belongs to the same family as ginger and turmeric, and is great in curries. Buy the seeds and grind them fresh.

Chilli: I've just planted a chilli in my herb garden and it's going gang-busters. If you're not a big chilli fan, but want some kick to your curry, try the milder, long cayenne chil-lies. If you're a veteran, the hotter, smaller bird's eye chillies or the eyeball-burning habaneros will be more your style.

Cinnamon: Ground cinnamon is delicious sprinkled on porridge or your homemade muesli mix.

Coriander: A favourite. Use leaves for salads and garnish for soups and curries; puree stalks and roots to make curry bases. Ground seeds are brilliant in any spice mix.

Curry leaf: A fresh herb that looks a bit like a lemon leaf and smells like curry. You can buy them fresh in large supermarkets.

Curry powder: A blend of ground coriander, turmeric, cumin, fenu-greek, chilli and other spices.

Dill: Fresh dill fronds look amazing as a garnish on everything from fish and eggs to vegetables. Dried dill is fine, too, if you can't find fresh.

Dukkah: A North African blend of roasted nuts, seeds and spices. Serve as a dip with olive oil or sprin-kle on roasted veggies or meat.

Galangal: This lovely spice tastes a bit like ginger and turmeric. It's avail-able ground in Asian grocers and is a key ingredient in Thai curries.

Ginger: I love this exotic flavour in smoothies. Fresh ginger is best and is easy to freeze, so you can grate it and have it whenever you need it.

Harissa paste: This fiery North Af-rican condiment made from chillies and ground spices is especially good with grilled or barbecued meat and fish, and roast veggies.

Kaffir lime leaves: Glossy, aromatic citrus leaf used in Asian dishes; you can buy them fresh in most super-markets and freeze them.

Mint: Mint leaves make a delicious herbal tea. Vietnamese mint has a stronger flavour and is very hardy if you want to grow some yourself.

Mustard: Yellow and brown mustard seeds are ground into powder, or preserved with lemon juice or vinegar.

Parsley: Regular parsley is amazing in tabbouleh, though I prefer flat-leaf for other dishes.

Pepper: I usually use freshly ground black pepper, though you can get white, pink and other colours.

Peri peri: This seasoning mix is made from crushed chillies, citrus peel, onion, salt, spices and herbs. Great with chicken!

Salt: I like to use sea salt and pink salt.

Sumac: This lovely, lemony red spice is made from ground sumac berries. It's delicious with grilled fish, chicken and seafood.

Turmeric: Turmeric is a major ingredient in Indian curries. It's related to ginger and you can buy the fresh root and use it in the same way if you like (use gloves unless you don't mind having bright orange hands). I use ground turmeric, which is perfectly fine.

Add delicious FLAVOUR BURSTS with HERBS and SPICES.

SHOULD YOU WORRY ABOUT SALT?

Everyone knows that too much salt increases our risk of developing high blood pressure, which can lead to heart disease. And dietary guidelines continue to advise that we reduce our salt intake. However, there's no need to get too panicky about adding a bit of salt to home-cooked meals. As long as you are not eating out much (I never add salt to any restaurant meal), and you are not buying greasy takeaway or processed foods, you are automatically reducing your salt intake by the container-load. So if you want a pinch of salt on your broccoli, by all means go for it.

OTHER NAMES FOR SALT

BAKING POWDER

BOOSTER

GARLIC, ONION OR CELERY SALT

MEAT OR YEAST EXTRACT

MONOSODIUM GLUTAMATE (MSG)

ROCK SALT

SEA SALT

SODIUM BICARBONATE

SODIUM METABISULPHATE

SODIUM NITRATE /NITRITE

STOCK

Water
& other drinks

Water is needed for most bodily functions – digestion, blood and the transportation of nutrients, the removal of waste and toxins, cushioning of tissues, organs and joints, regulating temperature, maintaining good skin and more. I always keep a jug of water in the fridge, sometimes with fresh mint leaves, or sliced lemon or cucumber.

How much water?

For a long time we were told to drink eight glasses of water (including tea, coffee and other drinks) per day, but this wasn't helpful. A man who weighs 150 kg is clearly not going to require the same amount of water as a 55 kg woman! Besides, a 'glass' can mean anything from 200 ml to 600 ml. The truth is we need approximately 30 ml of water per kilo of body weight per day for our usual body functions. So if you weigh 70 kg, you multiply 70 x 30 = 2100 ml or 2.1 litres. Of course, we need a lot more water if we are training, breastfeeding or on certain medications.

Like the majority of us, I have to admit I don't always drink enough water, particularly during winter. However, when I do, I notice that my skin is not as dry, nor is my scalp, and the extra trip or two to the bathroom could be considered 'incidental exercise' thus helping me burn up calories!

Interestingly, a lot of the times that I think I'm hungry I'm actually thirsty, and once I have glass of water, I'm no longer tempted to have an extra snack. If you're struggling to drink your quota, try adding a squeeze of lemon or lime juice, fresh berries or a sprig of mint. Having a bottle of water on your desk, in your car or in your handbag increases the likelihood of you reaching your daily target.

Juice

I never drink commercial fruit juices as they are usually full of sugar or other additives. Even freshly squeezed juice is high in calories, and I'd rather have the piece of fruit itself and get all the fibre as well. If I do have a juice it will always be a veggie juice (like carrot, ginger and mint) rather than a fruit juice.

Use a water bottle that you fill up from home. We don't need any more plastic bottles.

Tea & coffee

Green, black and white tea all come from the same plant and all have similar amounts of caffeine – they're just processed differently. Red tea or rooibos tea comes from a different plant and contains no caffeine. Herbal teas are made by brewing herbs, spices and the leaves and flowers of other plants in hot water. Unless they are mixed with regular tea, they shouldn't contain caffeine. Drinking tea is a great way to ensure you get your daily quota of water. I like earl grey, green, jasmine and peppermint.

I also love my morning coffee. Caffeine is basically a stimulant, increasing your heart rate and blood pressure, and releasing sugar into your bloodstream. This helps us to concentrate and elevates our mood, but it can also interfere with sleep, which is why I don't drink it at night. The half life of caffeine in the body is roughly 6 hours; so if you have a coffee in the afternoon, you'll still have half of that caffeine in your system at 10 o'clock.

Hundreds of studies have looked at the benefits of drinking coffee, some claiming it may help lower the risk of cardiovascular disease, diabetes, and even some forms of cancer. However, many are population-based observational studies, so researchers can't be sure the participants are doing something else that is reducing their risk of disease. Overall, I figure it can't hurt to drink a cup a day, and it might even be a good thing.

Try adding MINT leaves or fresh BERRIES for a flavour boost.

TEN HEALTHY EATING HABITS

I can bang on about the health benefits of wholefood until the cows come home, but it's not going to make you eat it! That's where you come in. You're the one who gets to make the choices. Some people like to blame the big food giants for helping to create the obesity epidemic; that our modern life is 'disempowering'. And yes, their shifty marketing practices in the face of all the evidence against sugar and dodgy oils remind me of the tactics of the tobacco industry. But focusing on these guys keeps you in a victim mentality, and hinders you from taking responsibility. You *do* have choices. And although it might take a bit more effort to source healthy ingredients and do a bit of cooking, you get to vote with your dollar. If enough of us stop buying their crappy, disease-causing foods it might encourage positive change. So hang in there. And remember: it's your thinking that is disempowering, the self-talk that drives your old habits.

Changing habits

Habits are nothing more than unquestioned behaviours – things we've been doing for ages that we can't seem to stop, like skipping breakfast, or having that 5 o'clock glass of wine. They feel easy and normal, as if they're part of who we are, and if we're honest, the idea of doing something different seems scary. So we come up with reasons why these habits are okay ('I deserve this'; 'I won't eat any dinner to make up for it') and we convince ourselves that it's too hard to change now. But I'm here to tell you that you *can* change your habits. I've done it myself, and I've helped thousands of people do it, so I know you can, too. It's all about questioning the thoughts and beliefs that underpin your behaviour – I sometimes call them excuses, because when it comes to health goals, that's what a lot of them are. You know the ones: 'I'm a terrible cook', or 'I'll always be fat', or 'I don't have time to cook', or 'My family won't eat veggies.'

Challenge your excuses

The first step is to identify these excuses by writing them down, and then give them a run for their money. Think of three examples for each excuse that prove the opposite and challenge your beliefs. For example, if one excuse is 'I am a terrible cook', your three opposites might be: 'I can make toast', 'I can cook pasta', 'I can grate carrots'. And if you can think of more, keep writing. It doesn't matter how minor the examples are: the point is that you are creating new thought patterns. Some people call this 'rewiring your brain'. However, sometimes our eating habits can be about something much deeper, such as numbing emotional pain or filling an emptiness in our lives. This is when we need to look within, and get help to change our thinking. Of course, this doesn't happen in an afternoon. It's taken years to attach to these beliefs and habits, so it will take persistence and consistency to form new ones.

Practise your new habits

The next step is to start showing yourself that you can do things a different way, that you are not trapped. Identify a habit that you want to adopt: for example, cleaning your teeth after dinner so that you don't eat anything else, or not having alcohol during the week. And start practising – consistently. Habits and consistency go hand in hand. And we all have the ability to be consistent. Think about it – we have consistently gone back for seconds and consistently bought a chocolate bar when filling up at the servo. We're fantastic at it! Now it's just a matter of being consistent with the right habits, the habits that will serve you and help you move forward. Sure, there will be days when you might slip up, but be kind to yourself. You're shifting behaviours that have received years and years of reinforcement. Don't let one mistake throw you off the horse. That's called being human, but it's also called playing the victim, throwing your arms up and chucking it in. Remember, we don't do victim.

   The following habits are the ones I have learned to use, and are the ones you can use, too. There are no miracles when it comes to improving your health and wellbeing, but you can take great joy in each of the steps you take to reach your goals.

There are NO MIRACLES when it comes to improving your HEALTH and WELLBEING. But you can take GREAT JOY in each of the steps you take.

PLAN YOUR MEALS

Being organised is probably the single most important element of good nutrition – seriously! Shop at least once a week if you can, and buy everything you need for the next week's meals. I always keep a shopping list on the go so I can restock the fridge, freezer or pantry when ingredients run low. This may sound over the top if you are used to making it up as you go along, but believe me, it's the reason so many people fall back on old habits like calling for pizza or heating up pies. If you are serious about managing your weight, you have to be prepared to put some time into shopping and cooking up a storm.

Now I'm not saying you have to stand at the stove for 2 hours every night – I haven't got time for that, and I'm sure you don't either. I like to prepare a couple of staples on the weekend for freezing or to use during the week, which cuts down my prep time on weeknights. Reheating leftovers is a big time-saver, but so is heating up some frozen frittata, soup or burger patties that I've thawed in the fridge over-night. You can be this efficient too – you only need to be prepared. Some people complain that they won't know what they'll feel like eating so far in advance, but that's just another excuse. As long as you know at the start of the day what you're going to be making that night for dinner, you can be prepared. If you don't have the ingredients in the house, don't worry – you can still grab them on the way home. But what you don't want to do is end up staring into an empty fridge saying 'What am I going to eat tonight . . .?'

When you are organised you are back in control. You aren't letting others be re-sponsible for what you eat. When you let go of that responsibility, when you let others determine how your body is nourished, managing your weight becomes a nightmare. See page 54 for more about meal plans and efficient shopping.

INTERMITTENT FASTING

Now I'm sure you've heard of the latest diet fad, intermittent fasting, where you either reduce your caloric intake to 500 calories for 2 days a week (the '5:2'), or you eat only between noon and 8 p.m. every day (the '16/8'). Personally, I don't mind it and I have done it as part of a healthy lifestyle: there's actually some pretty good science to back it up and, contrary to what we might think, people don't feel like bingeing on the day after they fast. However, the only way this kind of caloric restriction will work is if you eat nutrient-dense foods on your non-fasting days. If you chow down on junk food or drink your weight in beer on the other days, you won't see much improvement in either your weight or your health. Also, it's possible that this is just another way that food can hook into our reward pathways: 'If I'm a good girl and eat nothing today, I can have whatever I want tomorrow.' So by all means give it a go, but only if you are following the principles in this book and are addressing the nutritional value of what you are eating.

2.

EAT THREE MEALS A DAY

This is important to keep your metabolism running high. Your metabolism slows down when you sleep, not because you are sleeping, but because you are *not eating*, and it cranks up again when you tuck into a good brekkie. If you don't eat breakfast (you literally don't 'break' your 'fast'), your body slips into starvation mode, slowing your metabolism so that you conserve energy. Since your metabolism slows down without food, it makes sense to eat regularly during the day, but obviously *what* you eat is critical. It's got to be nutrient-dense food, not full of sugar and processed carbs, or you will be defeating the purpose.

Starting the day with a good breakfast also stops you playing games with yourself: 'If I skip breakfast and have an apple for lunch I'm allowed to stuff myself when I get home.' The number-one bad habit for nearly all of my overweight clients has been that they *don't eat breakfast*, barely eat lunch and then gorge themselves crazy from the moment they walk through the door in the evening until they go to bed.

Now this sounds like a lesson from the school of the bleeding obvious, but the best time to eat is *when we need the energy*, and for most of us that will be in the morning and perhaps at lunchtime depending on your job and daily activities. This is why your breakfast is *so* important – it needs to be a nutritious meal with some protein and complex carbohydrates to keep you going until lunchtime. Remember my mantra: 'Eat like a king for breakfast, a prince for lunch, and a pauper for dinner.' Plus, you'll sleep better when you don't have such a full stomach. Your children will also need snacks throughout the day, as will family members who do a lot of physical work or training.

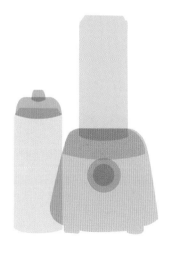

TIPS ON EATING REGULARLY

> *Get a smoothie maker with a jug* that doubles as a portable drink holder so that you can take your breakfast smoothie with you on the way to work.

> *Keep your kitchen stocked* with fresh ingredients.

> *Set your alarm for a bit earlier* or get your breakfast ready the night before (for example, if you like bircher muesli, soak it in the fridge overnight so it's ready to go).

> *Have leftovers in the fridge or meals in the freezer* ready for lunch, or do some prepping the night before (e.g. grate and wash some veggies to make a wrap or salad).

> *Brush your teeth straight after dinner* so you are not tempted to keep grazing until bedtime.

KICK SUGAR TO THE KERB

3

Earlier I talked about how sugar, not fat, is the main factor in our collectively expanding waistlines. And by 'sugar' I mean simple carbs in all of their forms. Everyday table sugar (sucrose) is half glucose and half fructose. Glucose is our body's primary energy source and as such can be metabolised by every organ of our bodies – our brain, our kidneys, our muscles – but fructose can only be metabolised by the liver which, put simply, converts it to fat. The process is a lot more complicated than that, but the upshot is that fructose not only makes us get fatter, faster, but also increases our risk of developing atherosclerosis (thickening of the arteries), high blood pressure, insulin resistance and diabetes.

Now this doesn't mean we can't eat fruit any more – we can, but we need to stick to just two serves a day. And forget about fruit juice – it's super-high in calories but has none of the fibre and nutrients you get from the flesh and skin.

Most of the extra sugar we ingest comes from the usual suspects: soft drinks, confectionery, chocolate, ice cream, biscuits, muffins, pies, pastries and cakes. These are all manufactured with a huge whack of sugar, usually 25–50 per cent (or even more in some cases). The rest is hidden in just about every processed food we buy: cereals, nut milks, sweetened yoghurt, bread, crackers, dips, spreads, sauce, mayo and dressings. And while you might think that you're okay with these foods since the sugar is in smaller amounts, it doesn't take long to add up.

DESSERTS & TREATS

As you know, I rarely eat dessert, and when I'm working with clients who need to lose a lot of weight, they don't either. However, this doesn't mean you can't have dessert or treats *ever again*! The word 'never' seems pretty extreme to me. It also sets us up to feel like complete failures if we can't live up to such unrealistic expectations. Plus, a treat doesn't have to mean empty calories – it can still contain lots of fibre, vitamins and nutrients. That's why I have included a treat section in this book, and why I haven't used refined sugar in any of the recipes. But please remember that you need to think of sweet foods as treats – to be indulged in only occasionally.

1. Be honest with yourself

The first step to cutting your sugar intake is to be honest about exactly how much you are having. I'm not talking about the sugar that is naturally found in dairy, veggies, fruit and nuts, but the sucrose and other sugars (see page 8) that are added to processed food. Keep a list of your sugar intake for one day. To do this, you'll need to look at the nutrition labels of everything you eat and drink. There is always a column that shows the sugar quantity per serve, and an indication of how much is in a serve. Add up all the sugar in grams, and then divide that by 5 to get the number of teaspoons. It should be under 10 teaspoons (preferably 5–6) for optimum health – far less if you are in the market for some serious weight loss.

2. Ditch the artificial sweeteners

To avoid the weight gain associated with high sugar intake, some people have foods artificially sweetened with saccharine, aspartame or sucralose. However, studies show that these substances still activate the brain's reward pathways and keep us hooked into seeking sweet things.

3. Make your own sauces and dressings

Most dressings, spreads, pastes and sauces have lots of added sugar. I've included recipes for tomato passata (see page 330), sweet chilli and other delicious dressings (see page 146) to help tame your sweet tooth.

4. Enjoy natural sweetness

As I explained earlier, we are biologically wired to seek out sweet stuff (our brains run on glucose). Yet, the amazing thing is that we can get all the glucose we need from the carbs in naturally sweet vegetables like carrots, beetroot, pumpkin, sweet potato and sweetcorn. We don't even need add to add extra sugar. And I promise you – when you start to cut down on sugar, you will actually taste the real flavour of these veggies, probably for the first time.

5. Revel in your self-control

Saying 'no' to offers of chocolate and cake can often get weird reactions from people around you, ranging from a high-five to shock to criticism. They might say things like, 'It can't hurt you', or 'You're taking this a bit far, aren't you?'

Being able to say no is one of the most important things you will ever learn – it puts you back in charge of your life and gives you the confidence to move forward. Anyway, you're not depriving yourself; you're giving yourself abundant life and health. And you're proving to yourself and everyone around you that you are in control.

MAKE VEGGIES THE ROCK STARS

4

The latest National Health and Medical Research Council dietary guidelines advise that adults need at least 5–6 serves of veggies and legumes every day (1 serve = 1 cup leafy greens or ½ cup other veggies and legumes like chickpeas) and 6 serves of grains or cereals (4 for menopausal women). But, importantly, it has *halved* the recommended serving sizes for grains/cereals (1 serve = 1 slice of bread or ½ cup cooked rice).

When I was growing up, it wasn't unusual to see people hoe into a large plate-sized steak with a big bowl of chips on the side where the only 'vegetable' was a dainty sprig of parsley. We now know that we had the proportions the wrong way around. Ratios for my evening meals will vary depending on the dish, but in general, veggies should take up three-quarters of the plate, and protein (from fish, meat, legumes, eggs or dairy) the other quarter. Breakfast and lunch is where you can include carbs from grain-based foods (oats, wholegrain or sourdough bread, wholemeal pasta, rice etc).

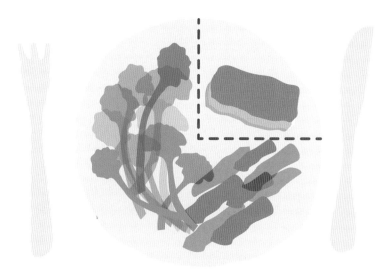

VEGGIES *should make up* THREE-QUARTERS
of your plate. MEAT, FISH, EGGS
or other PROTEIN *should take up*
the other QUARTER.

CONTROL YOUR PORTIONS

It's one thing to get your balance of protein, carbs and fats right, but another to manage the amount you eat. A lot of my clients have what I call portion distortion: they've been piling their plates for so long they don't realise how huge the portions are. One of the ladies in my 12WBT program was telling everyone how bountiful the meals are, and sometimes she couldn't even finish them. You can imagine how mortified she was when she learned she'd been reading the recipes as serving one, when they served two. To her credit, she started again and this time she got it right.

In my experience, the best way to control portion size is to count calories, especially if your goal is to lose weight. Broadly speaking, an adult bloke who wants to lose weight needs to take in around 1800 calories a day (3 x 450-calorie meals plus 450 calories in snacks, tea and coffee). When he is happy with his weight, a maintenance diet is around 2000 calories. Women generally have less muscle than men, so burn fuel less efficiently. For weight loss we should aim for 1200 calories a day (3 x 300-calorie meals plus 300 calories for snacks/drinks), and for weight main-tenance, 1500 calories. Note that teenage boys who play sport will need to eat more than their parents – at least 2500 calories a day with plenty of that energy coming from wholegrains. Active teenage girls, too, will need more than their mums.

Over the page, I've given you an idea of some calories counts. You'll need some kitchen scales to get a sense of your veg portions, but packaged meat is already weighed, so it's not too hard to work out what 100 g or 200 g portions look like. Bear in mind the figures are rough guides only, and the calorie content will vary depend-ing on how your meat and veg are cooked. It's not an exact science, but it's handy if you don't want to consult a calorie counter every 5 minutes.

Reducing your portions is going to be a little uncomfortable at first. You've trained your stomach to want *way* more than it needs, so it's probably going to let you know about it. But you won't die! You will still be filling your belly, but it will be with nutrient-dense, low-calorie foods rather than those with zero nutrients and a gazillion calories.

Never go back for seconds

When you serve the food you plan to eat, know that that's *it*. To stop yourself reaching for the serving spoon, tell yourself:

'These leftovers will be great for lunch tomorrow.'

'I have eaten enough.'

'I deserve to be fit and healthy.'

'I need to stop behaving like the neighbour's pet labrador.'

Now clear away the dishes, put the leftovers away and clean your teeth. Eating time is over.

Portion Control & Calories

The following is a *very* rough guide I use to work out portion sizes:

100 G 'GREENS' (lettuce, tomatoes, capsicum, bok choy, cabbage, broccoli, zucchini, eggplant)	20 CALORIES
100 G 'LIGHT' VEGETABLES (carrots, onions, swede, turnip, leeks)	30 CALORIES
100 G 'HEAVY' VEGETABLES (potato, sweet potato, pumpkin, parsnip, sweetcorn)	80 CALORIES
½ CUP COOKED WHOLEGRAIN BASMATI RICE	108 CALORIES
½ CUP COOKED WHOLEWHEAT PASTA	105 CALORIES
1 G WHITE FISH, SEAFOOD OR KANGAROO	1 CALORIE
1 G CHICKEN OR TUNA	1.5 CALORIES
1 G RED MEAT OR SALMON	2 CALORIES
1 LARGE EGG	90 CALORIES
½ CUP TINNED BEANS OR LENTILS	100 CALORIES
1 TEASPOON OLIVE OIL	40 CALORIES

You will still be FILLING YOUR BELLY, but it will be with NUTRIENT-DENSE, LOW-CALORIE foods.

6

EAT FOR NOURISHMENT, NOT COMFORT

I know only too well how food can be used as an anaesthetic, an antidepressant, a toast for celebration, a time-filler, a control mechanism, a diversion – anything besides actually satisfying genuine hunger. And what's even more bizarre is that many of us have forgotten what hunger is, and what it really feels like.

For many of us, eating and drinking are closely connected to our emotions, whether we are aware of it or not. We might reach for a glass of wine (or five) when we are feeling stressed or angry; hoe into a family block of chocolate when we feel down or lonely; or use coffee and cake as a reward for doing chores that we don't enjoy. This is emotional eating, and is rampant among my clients.

When you are emotional, do you tell yourself you'll feel better if you eat, whether you are hungry or not? And afterwards, do you feel worse because on top of your original feelings, you've now got a heap of guilt and shame?

The key to changing this eating pattern is to become aware of your triggers – to notice the thoughts that go through your head before you reach for the fridge door and to challenge them; 'I will *not* feel better if I eat this.' And to do something else, ideally something that makes you feel better about yourself:

> Call a friend.

> Go for a walk or a run.

> Weed the garden.

> Wash the dog.

> Clean something.

Reward yourself without using your stomach

Over the years, I've seen a stack of people work like demons in the gym and then undo all of their hard work by rewarding themselves with sugary, fatty foods. Although they might build some muscle and get fitter, they don't lose weight.

Food is nourishment. Every time you prepare a meal, think of it as an opportunity to take care of yourself; as a way of giving yourself the love you deserve. This might sound selfish, especially if you are used to putting everyone else first. In fact the opposite is true, because by looking after yourself, they get a better version of you – they get someone who feels happy about herself, and is kinder, patient and more generous – not the resentful version.

When you take positive steps towards your health goals, whether they be about weight loss, fitness or wellbeing, don't reward yourself with food. Put aside the money you save by not buying chocolates, junk food or wine, and use it to treat yourself in other ways:

> Have a massage, a manicure or get your hair done.

> Buy a new workout outfit or a Fitbit.

> Save it all up for a holiday or a retreat.

HOW TO ENCOURAGE HEALTHY EATING HABITS FOR YOUR KIDS

> **Never give children junk food as a reward** for good behaviour or to pacify bad behaviour. My view on this is clear-cut: I see it as a form of child abuse. You are setting up habits for a lifetime. Do you want your children to develop the habits you are working so hard to change? Be the one to break the cycle.

> **Never bribe children to eat their veggies by using dessert.** It teaches them that nutritious food is inferior to sugary food, and encourages them to develop an unhealthy relationship with crap food.

> **Don't ask your children, 'Do you want some broccoli?' Just serve it up** – they'll see green food as something normal that everyone has. The earlier you start them with these flavours the better. It's about being consistent even when you're knackered and they're begging for chicken nuggets.

> **Children's palates develop at different rates,** but sometimes it can take 10–15 tastes of something before they decide they like it. So offer children a little of everything that the grown-ups are eating and don't growl at them if they don't try it. If they are offered lots of different foods in a supportive environment, they are more likely to experiment with different flavours and textures.

> **Model healthy eating habits** – this is the most important strategy of all. Kids have an inbuilt bullshit detector, so if you're yelling at them to eat their veggies when you have barely eaten a stick of carrot they'll never buy it.

7

HAVE ALCOHOL-FREE DAYS

I'm no teetotaller, but I'm serious about looking after my body. Before I had my baby, these were my rules:

> Aim for at least 4–5 alcohol-free days a week.
> Never drink when I'm by myself.
> Never drink when I've had a hard day.
> Stop drinking after dinner.

Being able to moderate my drinking makes me feel like I'm in the driver's seat. I didn't drink at all when I was pregnant, and I'm not keen on drinking while breastfeeding either. The latest National Health and Medical Research Council guidelines now advise that pregnant women do not drink *any* alcohol; some beer labels now carry a little symbol of a pregnant woman skolling a bottle with a cross through it.

When it comes to maintaining a healthy weight, there are two reasons that alcohol is the enemy. The first is that beer goggles encourage stupid food choices – we're much more likely to reach for unhealthy foods when we've had a couple of drinks. This is because alcohol works on the dopamine system in our brains (the reward pathway), just like sugary and fatty foods do, so our bodies just want to keep partying.

The second reason is that the liver metabolises alcohol first, leaving any sugary food you've eaten to be stored for later (aka, as *fat*). The body treats alcohol as a toxin (it's where we get the word 'intoxicated'), so our livers immediately get to work on it to try to minimise its effects on the brain. (Alcohol depresses the central nervous system, messing with cognitive function, emotion regulation, sensory perception and physical coordination, among other things.)

If you choose to drink alcohol, the healthiest option is to limit your intake to one or two drinks once or twice a week. Also, keep away from top-shelf stuff that's served with sugary mixers. Maybe try a preservative-free red wine, or a vodka with fresh lime, mint and soda. And if you can't go 3 days without having a drink, you might need to do some soul-searching.

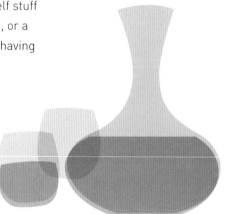

8.

EAT MINDFULLY

There are two ways to eat: consciously and unconsciously. When you eat consciously (mindfully), you are paying attention to the look, smell and taste of the food, and savouring each mouthful. When you eat unconsciously, you are shovelling the food in without really knowing what the hell it is – it could be deep-fried cardboard and it wouldn't even register.

There is some evidence that paying attention to the flavour and texture of the food you are eating and slowing the whole eating process right down may be helpful in portion control and maintaining a healthy weight. There is also evidence that mindfulness-based cognitive therapy can help obese people manage food cravings.

Years ago, parents used to exhort their children to 'chew your food properly', anything from 20–40 times (!). Weirdly, studies have shown that people do eat less if they count how many times they chew. But mindfulness is not the same thing. It's more about slowing down and noticing what you are experiencing and what is happening around you.

TIPS FOR MINDFUL EATING

> *Always eat at the dinner table. If you eat while driving, walking, watching TV, working, or standing in front of the fridge or pantry, it's harder for you to stay in control. It's no coincidence that many obese families don't have a dining table – they always eat on the couch.*

> *Minimise noise and distractions while you eat – no radio or TV blaring in the background and no electronic devices at the table. Sharing food as a family keeps you connected, teaches your children about taking turns to talk and listen, and gives them some basic rules of etiquette.*

> *Put your food on a plate, no matter how small the serve. This encourages you to pay attention to how much you are eating.*

> *Never eat food that comes in bags, boxes or cartons (aka most fast food) – reaching into the dark depths encourages unconscious zombie munching.*

> *Learn to say 'no'. Some people feel guilty if they don't accept that packet of plastic food on the plane trip, a slice of birthday cake at the office, or the dessert at a friend's dinner party. Simply say, 'No, thank you'. It's your body. You don't need to give a reason, even if they ask.*

PUT SLEEP BEFORE FOOD

Along with not having breakfast, the majority of my obese clients also share another bad habit: staying up very late and grazing until they go to bed. Yet sleep is *incredibly* important to our health – without enough of it we can't concentrate, our short-term memory is affected and physically we're clumsy and have poor reaction times. Severe sleep deprivation leads to hallucinations and even psychosis (it has long been used as a form of torture).

But there's another reason sleep is crucial. If you don't get enough uninterrupted sleep, your body releases the stress hormone cortisol, which boosts your appetite (so your body has the extra energy it needs to get through such a long day). But at the same time, lack of sleep leads to lower levels of leptin (the hormone that tells your brain you're full), leaving you even more susceptible to overeating.

You need 7–8 hours sleep every night to function properly and to give yourself the best chance of managing your weight.

TIPS FOR GETTING A GOOD NIGHT'S SLEEP

> ***Go to bed earlier*** *so that you give yourself the best change of getting 7–8 hours sleep.*

> ***Go to bed at the same time every night****, give or take half an hour, as this helps your body clock.*

> ***Avoid caffeine, alcohol or food within 4 hours*** *of bedtime – they all disrupt sleep.*

> ***Avoid intense exercise within 2 hours*** *of going to bed.*

> ***Make sure your bed is comfortable****.*

> ***Make sure your room is cool*** *(16–18 degrees Celsius is ideal).*

> ***Make your room as dark*** *as possible, as this helps your body clock.*

> ***Keep electronic equipment out*** *of your bedroom.*

> ***Practise a pre-sleep ritual****, such as a relaxation technique, so that your body knows to wind down.*

10. UNPLUG YOURSELF REGULARLY

I know this sounds like it has nothing to do with food, but turning off your phone every now and again and unplugging yourself from the madness is really important for your health. This is because stress and being overweight are very closely linked. When we are under stress, our adrenal gland pumps out adrenaline (the 'fight or flight' hormone that elevates heart rate, blood pressure and respiration in readiness for action), and cortisol, which is involved in glucose metabolism and blood sugar maintenance, as well as inflammatory response and immune function.

Unlike adrenaline, which is produced in short bursts, cortisol can be elevated for long periods, and one of the things it does is increase abdominal fat. From a survival point of view, this emergency fat storage is designed to keep us alive if we have to endure harsh conditions for long periods. The problem is, we're leading sedentary lives and most of the stress is in our heads – worrying about things we can't control or getting angry when things don't go our way. (This is one reason we need to exercise regularly: when we're busy concentrating on not falling over, or trying to catch our breath, we give our minds a rest.) But for most of us, our modern way of life means that our cortisol levels get pumped up so many times during our busy days that it doesn't get much chance to return to normal, and we're not burning any of the extra fat that's being stored in the process. So we get bigger and unhappier, and we don't know how to break the cycle. This is why it's so important to find something in your life that helps you to de-stress, and to give yourself permission to do it.

TIPS FOR DE-STRESSING

For me, being able to get stuff done around the house is important for maintaining a positive headspace. Once I tick a couple of things off my to-do list, I feel I can really relax. Other ways I chill that you might want to try:

> ***Block out some time for yourself,*** *even if it's just half an hour, and do something that you really love: go for a walk, read, meditate or just sit and stare into space (I'm really good at that one).*

> ***Plan to do something different*** *and maybe even a bit challenging that sounds like fun. We recently invested in stand-up paddle-boards – and we love it.*

> ***Get out of the city as often as you can.*** *When I do, it does me the world of good. I love how the pace slows right down – it's so calming.*

> ***Do something active in nature.*** *We try to go for a hike in a national park whenever we can.*

AN ORGANISED KITCHEN

*n*ow that you've got the lowdown on nutrient-dense food, and
how to create new habits around getting it into your belly, I want
to give you a few tips on stocking your kitchen and cooking efficiently
before we get into the recipes. In this section, I show you what healthy,
real-food shopping looks like and suggest some of my favourite pantry,
fridge and freezer staples, plus there are five different meal plans and
accompanying shopping lists.

Where you choose to buy your produce and groceries is up to you,
but I try to get to a farmers' market as often as I can. I know the fruit and
vegetables are fresh, local and seasonal (which ticks all of my sustainability boxes), and it's great to be able to talk to the farmers and find out about
how they grow and harvest them. Take your kids along so that they learn
stuff, too. Local greengrocers are also excellent, and will be able to tell
you if their suppliers use organic farming methods. Another option is to
do your shopping online. This can be a life saver if you're time poor, have a
football team of kids who make shopping hell, or you want to minimise the
temptation of the chocolate aisle.

Part of being ORGANISED is being more EFFICIENT in the way you prepare meals.

Part of being organised is being more efficient in the way you prepare
meals. I always try to cook efficiently by making more than one meal at
once. By doubling the quantities, for example, I can cook two meals, one
to be eaten right away and the other frozen or refrigerated for later.

Another option is to simply cook some extra ingredients to use as
the basis for another meal. For example, sometimes I partly steam some
extra vegetables so I can bake them the next night with some fish (and
they take the same amount of time to cook), or I roast a few extra veggies
on the barbecue to add to a salad for the next day.

SHOPPING TIPS

▶ Keep a shopping list in a
visible place and add to it
as you run out of staples.

▶ Pick some recipes and
do a stocktake of your
pantry/fridge/freezer,
adding ingredients you
need to get.

▶ Remember to take your
list with you!

TIPS FOR HAPPY COOKING

▶ Think of cooking as a fun hobby, not a chore. Put music on; get the family involved.

▶ Choose simple recipes if you're just starting out.

▶ Take photos of meals you've prepared that you are proud of, or even your disasters so that you can see how far you've come.

▶ Don't be afraid to experiment: most of my recipes have lots of different options so you can find something that fits your tastes.

Eat a RAINBOW of FRUIT and VEGETABLES.

They're jam-Packed with VITAMINS and MINERALS.

LENTILS, BEANS
and CHICKPEAS
are cheap, versatile
and nutritious.

NUTS and SEEDS are NUTRITIONAL POWERHOUSES.

DAIRY foods are rich in CALCIUM and PROTEIN.

OLIVE OIL
and AVOCADO
are great
HEALTHY FATS.

WHOLEGRAINS are an
excellent source of ENERGY.

SEAFOOD, POULTRY and RED MEAT are staple sources of PROTEIN.

IN THE PANTRY
↓

Kitchen Staples

- capers
- coconut cream
- light coconut milk
- miso paste
- mustard: dijon; wholegrain
- nori (seaweed) sheets
- tahini (unhulled)
- tamari (gluten-free soy sauce)
- tinned red salmon
- tinned tuna in springwater
- tomato passata (see page 330); tomato paste
- vinegar: balsamic; red wine; white wine

Oils
- avocado oil
- coconut oil and cooking spray
- extra virgin olive oil and cooking spray
- extra light olive oil
- macadamia oil
- sesame oil

Grains, lentils & beans
- bread: rice mountain bread; rye sourdough
- couscous (wholemeal)
- noodles: brown rice vermicelli; soba
- oats: quick; rolled
- pasta (wholemeal)
- polenta
- rice: brown basmati; puffed; wild
- lentils: brown; dried split red
- beans: black; butter; cannellini; red kidney
- chickpeas

Nuts, seeds & dried fruit
- almonds: whole; flaked; slivered; almond meal; almond spread
- brazil nuts
- cashews
- coconut: flaked; shredded, desiccated; coconut flour
- hazelnuts
- macadamias
- pecans
- pine nuts
- pistachios
- walnuts
- chia seeds
- linseeds
- pumpkin seeds
- sesame seeds
- sunflower seeds
- quinoa: flakes; puffed; seeds
- craisins (dried cranberries)
- freeze-dried strawberries

Herbs & spices
- sea salt
- pepper: cracked black; ground white
- dried mixed herbs
- allspice
- cajun seasoning
- cayenne pepper
- cinnamon: ground; sticks
- coriander: ground; seeds
- cumin: ground; seeds
- curry powder
- chilli flakes
- dukkah
- fennel seeds
- mixed spice
- mustard seeds
- nutmeg
- oregano
- paprika
- saffron
- sumac
- turmeric

Baking & sweet treats
- baking powder
- bicarbonate of soda
- dark chocolate (70–80 per cent cocoa)
- flours: arrowroot (tapioca flour), cornflour; rice flour; self-raising wholemeal; plain wholemeal
- honey
- pure maple syrup
- raw cacao powder
- unsweetened apple puree
- vanilla bean paste or extract

IN THE FRIDGE

- butter
- cheese: cheddar; cottage; Danish feta; parmesan; ricotta
- eggs
- Fermented Slaw (see page 332)
- Labne (see page 333)
- milk: unsweetened almond milk; rice milk
- olives: green; kalamata
- stock: chicken; vegetable (see page 331)
- tofu: firm
- yoghurt: full-cream Greek

IN THE FREEZER

- blueberries; mixed berries; raspberries
- baby peas
- edamame (soybean pods)

Some of my favourite PANTRY, FRIDGE and FREEZER STAPLES.

Meal Plans

The following meal plans are there to help you work out how to structure your meals, particularly if you are in the process of changing the way you and your family eat. Depending on whether or not you want to lose or maintain weight, or feed your growing family or just get healthy, you can adjust as needed.

I want to point out straight up that I don't personally count calories. Over the years I've honed my skills around understanding nutrition, best choices and portion size. I've been doing it for years and it comes as naturally to me as breathing. However, when I first start working with clients they usually need some guidelines and parameters to work with, as often they are completely unsure of where and how to begin. We start with an understanding of food, how it works, best choices, worst choices and, of course, portion control. Part of the learning is about calories, as once someone gets a handle on how many calories are in

certain foods, the penny drops as to why they haven't been able to lose the weight or change their shape, fitness or health. They also learn very quickly why they are still on the merry-go-round even though they may have been eating fairly healthily: because their portion sizes have been so heavy-handed their calorie intake is still too high. It gives people a visual 'on the plate' or 'in the bowl', which they can later use as a tool rather than counting calories. It's a first step towards being able to know the best choices, then how much is enough on the plate, to eventually it all becoming second nature. It's all about learning. Learning about food and how it works for you, learning about best choices, learning about portions, learning how to put together incredibly delicious and nutritious meals, and learning about the joy of food!

For those wanting to lose weight, I recommend approximately 1200 calories a day for women and 1800

calories for men. Many of the meals listed here are about 300 calories or less per portion (so the base is for those trying to lose weight). The idea is that once you know what 300 calories looks like, you can build on this, depending on your and your family's needs. My theory is that it's easier in every way to add rather than subtract when it comes to food (if it's there we'll eat it!). To get to the 1200 calories recommended for weight loss, or to get the calorie intake that's right for you, select more energy-dense snacks and/or increase the portion sizes of your meals.

If it was me, I'd be going for the portion-size increase. I am not a big snacker these days and after years of trial and error, I am pretty good at knowing the portion size I need, and I tend to stick to three good-sized meals. But everyone is different, and you will need to adjust and experiment as you go along. What I do know is this. If you get used to eating nutrient-dense, non-processed food you will find it gets easier to know what works for you in terms of losing or maintaining a healthy weight – and you'll feel great!

Active Family PLAN

	MONDAY	TUESDAY	WEDNESDAY	THURSDAY	FRIDAY
BREAKFAST	No-bake Granola (page 91) 173/serve + ½ cup unsweetened almond milk 15/serve	*2 x quantity* Zucchini, Ham & Cheddar Muffins (page 96) 360/serve (3 muffins)	*leftovers* No-bake Granola 173/serve + ½ cup unsweetened almond milk 15/serve	Raspberry, Coconut & Dark Choc Loaf (page 95) 238/serve	Vegetable Corn… (page 101) 300/serve (2 pie… + Speck & Tom… Fritatta (page… 196/serve
SNACK	Raw Carrot Cake (page 299) 476/serve	*leftovers* Lunchbox Oat Slice 220/serve	*leftovers* Zucchini, Ham & Cheddar Muffins 360/serve	Spiced Tamari Edamame (page 243) 133/serve + Baked Herb Ricotta 185/serve	Dried Trail M… (page 242) 189/serve
LUNCH	Chicken Caesar Wrap (page 156) 263/serve	Israeli Couscous Salad (page 142) 169/serve	Chinese Cabbage Wraps (page 154) 208/serve	Beef & Beetroot on Rye (page 168) 339/serve	Macerated Tomatoes wi… Broken Pas… (page 163) 170/serve
SNACK	Lunchbox Oat Slice (page 266) 220/serve	*leftovers* Raw Banoffee Pie 294/serve	*leftovers* Lunchbox Oat Slice 220/serve	Ricotta Whip (page 272) 89/serve	*2 x quantity* Blueberry … Banana Smoo… (page 89) 178/serve
DINNER	Stir-fried Broccoli & Cashew Chicken (page 202) 203/serve + ½ cup cooked brown basmati rice 94/serve	Broccoli & Lamb Kofta with Herby Beetroot Salad (page 200) 192/serve	Mexican Black Beans (page 227) 317/serve	Zucchini & Fennel Chicken Loaf (page 182) 239/serve	Garlic Mushroom… Celeriac Smas… Peppered Ste… (page 189) 249/serve
TREAT	Raw Banoffee Pie (page 319) 294/serve	Beetroot Fudge Brownie (page 323) 198/serve (2 pieces)	Tropical Frozen Yogurt (page 294) 275/serve (divide by 4 instead of 6)	*leftovers* Beetroot Fudge Brownie 198/serve	Choc-banan… Pops (page 2… 275/serve (2 pieces ea…
ADDITIONAL SNACK TREAT	Tuna & Wild Rice Slice (page 254) 130/serve (1 piece) + Sesame Cucumber 'Nuggets' (page 257) 55/serve	*leftovers* Tuna & Wild Rice Slice 130/serve + Sesame Cucumber 'Nuggets' 55/serve	Baked Herb Ricotta (page 239) 185/serve (5 mini muffins)	Parmesan Vegetable Fries (page 246) 97/serve	Baked Herb Ri… 185/serve
	1923	1618	1753	1518	1742

SATURDAY	SUNDAY
...nana Pancakes ...h Pineapple & ...rawberry Salsa (page 70) ...174/serve	Baked Ratatouille Eggs (page 102) 153/serve
...piced Tamari Edamame 133/serve	*leftovers* Dried Trail Mix 189/serve + Tuna & Wild Rice Slice 130/serve
...auliflower & ...roccoli Fried ...ce' (page 151) 127/serve	Hearty Chicken & Risoni Soup (page 126) 243/serve
leftovers ...w Carrot Cake 476/serve	*leftovers* Vegetable Cornbread (toasted) 300/serve
Vegetable ...paghetti with ...ked Meatballs (page 218) 387/serve	Italian Roast Capsicum with Snapper & Wild Rice Crumb (page 186) 322/serve
...trawberries & ...Coco-cream (page 302) 250/serve	*leftovers* Raw Banoffee Pie 294/serve
...& Wild Rice Slice 130/serve ...same Cucumber 'Nuggets' 55/serve	Cauliflower Dip with Cumin (page 262) 85/serve + Sesame Cucumber 'Nuggets' 55/serve
1732	1771

SHOPPING LIST

VEG & FRUIT
10 garlic cloves
3 cm piece ginger
1 small red onion
11 spring onions
4 golden shallots
4 celery stalks
1 leek
400 g broccoli
1 bunch broccolini
1 bunch Chinese broccoli
1 bunch watercress
½ Chinese cabbage (wombok)
150 g baby spinach leaves
1 butter lettuce
1 small iceberg lettuce
2 baby cos lettuce
200 g mixed green salad leaves
80 g bean sprouts
375 g cherry tomatoes
400 g mixed baby tomatoes
2 tomatoes
4 radishes
19 Lebanese cucumbers
1 bunch baby beetroot
2 bunches mixed baby carrots
13 carrots
2 beetroot
2 parsnips
300 g celeriac
800 g cauliflower
2 red capsicums
3 green capsicums
1 yellow capsicum
2 corn cobs
2 baby eggplants
19 zucchini
250 g portobello mushrooms
150 g mixed exotic mushrooms
200 g swiss brown mushrooms
100 g snow peas
1½ lemons
1 lime
⅓ cup pomegranate seeds
2 oranges
125 g raspberries
1 kg small strawberries
14 bananas
1 mango
4 passionfruit
300 g pineapple
28 medjool dates

FRESH HERBS
basil
chives
coriander
flat-leaf parsley
lemon thyme
mint
rosemary
thyme
micro herbs (optional)
2 small red chillies
2 long red chillies
1 long green chilli

BUTCHER
2 chicken thigh fillets
300 g lamb mince
200 g cooked chicken
300 g skinless chicken breast
  fillets
400 g beef rump
200 g chicken mince
400 g trimmed beef sirloin
300 g beef mince
150 g sliced rare roast beef
50 g speck
150 g shaved ham
50 g shaved turkey

FISHMONGER
100 g raw prawn meat
4 x 100 g dory fillets, skinned
  and boned
300 g peeled cooked jumbo
  prawns

DELI/OTHER
200 g Israeli couscous
100 g angel hair pasta
8 baby bocconcini
250 ml buttermilk
50 g semi-dried tomato strips
wasabi
kewpie (Japanese mayo)
Mexican spice seasoning
lemon pepper seasoning
pure icing sugar

+ KITCHEN STAPLES
(pages 58-9)

AN ORGANISED KITCHEN

Simple Single PLAN

	MONDAY	TUESDAY	WEDNESDAY	THURSDAY	FRIDAY	SATURDAY	SUNDAY
BREAKFAST	½ x quantity recipe No-bake Granola (page 91) 173/serve + ½ cup unsweetened almond milk 15/serve	½ x quantity recipe Rosewater Citrus & Berries (page 80) 180/serve	leftovers Rosewater Citrus & Berries 180/serve	leftovers No-bake Granola 173/serve + ½ cup unsweetened almond milk 15/serve	leftovers No-bake Granola 173/serve + ½ cup unsweetened almond milk 15/serve	½ x quantity recipe Sumac Roasted Beets & Tomatoes with Fried Egg (page 111) 133/serve	½ x quantity recipe Vegetable Baked Beans (page 112) 296/serve
LUNCH	leftovers Yakitori Vegetable & Tofu Skewers (page 209) 132/serve	leftovers Stir-fried Broccoli & Cashew Chicken 203/serve + ½ cup cooked brown basmati rice 94/serve	leftovers Green Dhal 267/serve	leftovers Chilli Green Beans with Pork 114/serve	leftovers Green Alfredo Fettucine 221/serve	Fluffy Omelette with Brussels Sprouts (page 149) 269/serve	leftovers Sumac Roasted Beets & Tomatoes with Fried Egg 133/serve
DINNER	½ x quantity recipe Stir-fried Broccoli & Cashew Chicken (page 202) 203/serve + ½ cup cooked brown basmati rice 94/serve	½ x quantity recipe Green Dhal (page 211) 267/serve	½ x quantity recipe Chilli Green Beans with Pork (page 194) 114/serve	½ x quantity recipe Green Alfredo Fettucine (page 229) 221/serve	½ x quantity recipe Golden Tagine (page 214) 301/serve	leftovers Golden Tagine 301/serve	½ x quantity recipe Yakitori Vegetable & Tofu Skewers 132/serve
	617	744	561	523	710	703	561

A NOTE ABOUT THIS MEAL PLAN

This meal plan gives you the building blocks for a day's eating, but does not represent the total number of calories you'll need (1200 to 1500 for women; 1800 to 2000 for men); see page 45 for recommended daily calorie counts. If you are a snacker, build up your calories with snacks from the list opposite. If you prefer to eat three times a day, like I do, add a smoothie of your choice to your breakfast (see pages 86–7), then build up your calories at lunch and dinner by adding a salad (see pages 134–5) or a little bit of extra carb (rice or pasta), or green or starchy veg and/or protein (see page 47 for portion sizes). Alternatively, just increase the portion size of the above meals.

Avo Smash with Beetroot (page 236)	64/serve
Dried Trail Mix (page 242)	189/serve
Cottage Cheese Lettuce Wraps (page 255)	29/serve
Sesame Cucumber 'Nuggets' (page 257)	55/serve
Zucchini Hummus with Crackers (page 258)	324/serve
Mocha Frappe (page 270)	26/serve
Oven Dried Fruit (page 275)	80/serve
Berry Sorbet (page 292)	84/serve
Beetroot Fudge Brownie (page 323)	99/serve

VEG & FRUIT
4 garlic cloves
2 cm piece ginger
1 onion
½ white onion
½ small red onion
1 celery stalk
2 roma tomatoes
1 tomato
125 g cherry tomatoes
½ iceberg lettuce
½ bunch baby bok choy
6 Brussels sprouts
50 g green cabbage
½ bunch Chinese broccoli
1 bunch broccolini
100 g baby spinach leaves
½ bunch asparagus
1 red capsicum
250 g green beans
1½ zucchini
½ carrot
2 baby beetroot
1 baby fennel bulb
65 g blueberries
65 g raspberries
125 g strawberries
1 orange
½ large lemon
½ ruby grapefruit

FRESH HERBS
basil
chives
coriander
curry leaves
flat-leaf parsley
oregano
rosemary
thyme
1 long red chilli

BUTCHER
75 g pork mince
150 g skinless chicken breast
  fillet

FISHMONGER
250 g firm white fish fillets,
  skinned and boned

DELI/OTHER
25 g fresh seaweed salad
Chinese cooking wine
mirin
sake
Sriracha chilli sauce
teriyaki sauce
rosewater

+ KITCHEN STAPLES
(pages 58-9)

Energy-Booster PLAN

	MONDAY	TUESDAY	WEDNESDAY	THURSDAY	FRIDAY	SATURDAY	SUNDAY
BREAKFAST	Baked Porridge* (page 77) 143/serve	Spinach & Fennel Pikelets with Bacon (page 122) 239/serve	Gluten-free Bircher Bowls (page 88) 279/serve	Spinach & Fennel Pikelets with Bacon 239/serve	Baked Porridge* 143/serve	Vegetable Baked Beans (page 112) 296/serve	Banana Pancakes with Pineapple & Strawberry Salsa (page 78) 174/serve
LUNCH	Butter Bean & Tomato Soup (page 132) 330/serve	Beef & Beetroot on Rye (page 168) 339/serve	Vietnamese Coconut Pancakes with Shredded Pork (page 153) 197/serve	Peri Peri Potato Salad (page 137) 231/serve	Chicken Caesar Wrap (page 156) 263/serve	Beef & Beetroot on Rye 339/serve	Peri Peri Potato Salad 231/serve
DINNER	Vegetable Spaghetti with Baked Meatballs (page 218) 387/serve	Italian Roast Capsicum with Snapper & Wild Rice Crumb (page 186) 322/serve	Mexican Black Beans (page 227) 317/serve	Lentil-naise Marinara Parcels (page 215) 408/serve	Vegetable Spaghetti with Baked Meatballs 387/serve	Vegetable Lasagne* (page 226) 305/serve	Eggplant, Cauliflower & Kangaroo Moussaka* (page 220) 222/serve
	860	900	793	878	793	940	627

A NOTE ABOUT THIS MEAL PLAN

This meal plan gives you the building blocks for a day's eating, but does not represent the total number of calories you'll need (1200 to 1500 for women; 1800 to 2000 for men); see page 45 for recommended daily calorie counts. If you are a snacker, build up your calories with snacks from the list opposite. If you prefer to eat three times a day, like I do, add a smoothie of your choice to your breakfast (see pages 86–7), then build up your calories at lunch and dinner by adding a salad (see pages 134–5) or a little bit of extra carb (rice or pasta), or green or starchy veg and/or protein (see page 47 for portion sizes). Alternatively, just increase the portion size of the above meals.

Tahini & Mango Smoothie (page 89)	115/serve
Ultra Chocolate Smoothie (page 89)	166/serve
Blueberry & Banana Smoothie (page 89)	178/serve
Parmesan Vegetable Fries (page 246)	97/serve
Tuna & Wild Rice Slice (page 254)	130/serve
Zucchini Hummus with Crackers (page 258)	324/serve
Apple Nut Butter Sandwiches (page 263)	116/serve
Lunchbox Oat Slice (page 266)	220/serve
Ricotta Whip (page 272)	89/serve

*Serves 6; use leftovers for snack option

VEG & FRUIT
6 garlic cloves
1 onion
3 red onions
8 golden shallots
7 spring onions
8 celery stalks
500 g grape tomatoes
2 roma tomatoes
2 tomatoes
40 g baby spinach leaves
1 bunch English spinach
1 bunch watercress
250 g mixed salad leaves
4 large butter lettuce leaves
80 g bean sprouts
11 carrots
1 kg baby red potatoes

600 g cauliflower
400 g butternut pumpkin
2 large beetroot
2 bulbs baby fennel
14 zucchini
1 eggplant
3 red capsicums
3 green capsicums
1 yellow capsicum
1 corn cob
300 g green beans
250 g strawberries
1 orange
300 g pineapple
2 bananas
1 green apple
8 seedless red grapes
8 seedless green grapes
3 lemons
3 limes

FRESH HERBS
basil
chives
coriander
flat-leaf parsley
lemon thyme
micro herbs (optional)
mint
rosemary
Thai basil
2 small red chillies

BUTCHER
400 g beef rump steak
2 rindless bacon rashers
600 g beef mince
300 g kangaroo mince
50 g shaved leg ham
300 g finely sliced rare roast
  beef
150 g slow-cooked shredded
  pork
600 g cooked chicken

FISHMONGER
4 x 100 g dory fillets
400 g raw seafood marinara
  mix

DELI/OTHER
16 baby bocconcini
185 g fresh lasagne sheets
nutritional yeast
peri peri seasoning

+ KITCHEN STAPLES
(pages 58-9)

Immunity-Support PLAN

	MONDAY	TUESDAY	WEDNESDAY	THURSDAY	FRIDAY	SATURDAY	SUNDAY
BREAKFAST	Breakfast Greens with Spiced Chickpeas (page 121) 182/serve	Rosewater Citrus & Berries with Yoghurt (page 80) 180/serve	Pumpkin & Celeriac Rosti (page 107) 108/serve	Dill-pickled Mushrooms & Glazed Sprouts (page 113) 260/serve	Breakfast Greens with Spiced Chickpeas 182/serve	Rosewater Citrus & Berries with Yoghurt 180/serve	Pumpkin & Celeriac Rosti 108/serve
LUNCH	Roast Winter Vegetable & Bacon Soup (page 133) 181/serve	Fluffy Omelette with Brussels Sprouts (page 149) 269/serve	Hearty Chicken & Risoni Soup (page 126) 243/serve	Pickled Onion & Silverbeet with Sardines (page 173) 160/serve	Cajun roast Pumpkin & Quinoa Salad (page 157) 204/serve	Roast Winter Vegetable & Bacon Soup 181/serve	Pickled Onion & Silverbeet with Sardines 160/serve
DINNER	Super Greens & Salmon Bake with Cauliflower Crumb (page 197) 289/serve	Broccoli & Lamb Kofta with Herby Beetroot Salad (page 200) 192/serve	Green Dhal (page 211) 267/serve	Poached Spring Vegetables with Crispy Skin Chicken (page 181) 238/serve	Super Greens & Salmon Bake with Cauliflower Crumb 289/serve	Garlic Mushroom, Celeriac Smash & Peppered Steak (page 189) 249/serve	Poached Spring Vegetables with Crispy Skin Chicken 238/serve
	652	641	618	658	675	610	506

A NOTE ABOUT THIS MEAL PLAN

This meal plan gives you the building blocks for a day's eating, but does not represent the total number of calories you'll need (1200 for women and 1800 for men); see page 45 for recommended daily calorie counts. If you are a snacker, build up your calories with snacks from the list opposite. If you prefer to eat three times a day, like I do, add a smoothie of your choice to your breakfast (see pages 86–7), then build up your calories at lunch and dinner by adding a salad (see pages 134–5), or green or starchy veg and/or protein (see page 47 for portion sizes). Alternatively, just increase the portion size of the above meals.

Orange & Spinach Smoothie (page 89)	76/serve
Watercress & Cherry Smoothie (page 89)	99/serve
Avo Smash with Beetroot (page 236)	64/serve
Fresh Trail Mix (page 240)	40/serve
Green Goodness Soup (page 244)	133/serve
Cauliflower & Broccoli Popcorn (page 249)	59/serve
Cauliflower Dip with Cumin (page 262)	85/serve
Apple Nut Butter Sandwiches (page 263)	116/serve
Sweet Turmeric Milk (page 279)	70/serve

VEG & FRUIT
15 garlic cloves
2 cm piece ginger
1 onion
2 small red onions
2 spring onions
1 leek
1 broccoli
450 g small Brussels sprouts
3 bunches kale
2 bunches silverbeet
2 baby bok choy
2 bunches rainbow chard
400 g green cabbage
4 bunches English spinach
150 g baby spinach leaves
½ iceberg lettuce
100 g red cabbage
1.3 kg butternut pumpkin
500 g Kent pumpkin
4 parsnips
2 swedes
2 turnips
8 carrots
4 bunches heirloom baby
  carrots
1 bunch baby beetroot
1 kg celeriac
800 g cauliflower
300 g button mushrooms
250 g portobello mushrooms
150 g mixed exotic
  mushrooms
200 g swiss brown
  mushrooms
2 zucchini
200 g baby beans
300 g asparagus
160 g fresh peas
250 g blueberries
250 g raspberries
500 g strawberries
4 oranges
2 ruby grapefruit
1 pomegranate
6 lemons
2 limes

FRESH HERBS
basil
bay leaves
chives
coriander
curry leaves
dill
flat-leaf parsley
French tarragon
lemon thyme
mint
rosemary
thyme
1 long green chilli

BUTCHER
2 chicken thigh fillets, skin
  removed
800 g chicken thigh fillets,
  skin on
4 rindless streaky bacon
  rashers
400 g trimmed beef sirloin
300 g lamb mince

FISHMONGER
16 fresh whole sardines
600 g salmon fillet, skin and
  bones removed

DELI/OTHER
24 white anchovy fillets
110 g risoni
rosewater

+ KITCHEN STAPLES
(pages 58-9)

Weight-loss PLAN

	MONDAY	TUESDAY	WEDNESDAY	THURSDAY	FRIDAY	SATURDAY	SUNDAY
BREAKFAST	Kiwi & Avocado Smoothie (page 89) 145/serve	Spring Vegetable Frittata* (page 114) 135/serve	Peachy Cream Smoothie (page 89) 230/serve	Pumpkin & Celeriac Rosti (page 107) 108/serve	Kiwi & Avocado Smoothie (page 89) 145/serve	Sweet Potato & Salmon Frittata* (page 114) 161/serve	Blueberry & Banana Smoothie (page 89) 178/serve
LUNCH	Sushi Salad Bowl (page 141) 301/serve	Gingered Kale & Asparagus Stir-fry with Sichuan Beef (page 166) 120/serve	Cajun roast Pumpkin & Quinoa Salad (page 157) 204/serve	Roast Fennel & Carrot Salad with Goat's Cheese (page 145) 187/serve	Pickled Onion & Silverbeet with Sardines (page 173) 160/serve	Cauliflower & Broccoli Fried 'Rice' (page 151) 127/serve	Fluffy Omelette with Brussels Sprouts (page 149) 269/serve
DINNER	Poached Spring Vegetables with Crispy Skin Chicken (page 181) 238/serve	Brocco-Flower Pizza with Topping One (page 190) 277/serve	Super Greens & Salmon Bake with Cauliflower Crumb (page 197) 289/serve	Stir-fried Broccoli & Cashew Chicken (page 202) 203/serve	Vegetable Spaghetti with Baked Meatballs (page 218) 387/serve	Poached Spring Vegetables with Crispy Skin Chicken 238/serve	Super Greens & Salmon Bake with Cauliflower Crumb 289/serve
	684	532	723	498	692	526	736

A NOTE ABOUT THIS MEAL PLAN

This meal plan gives you the building blocks for a day's eating, but does not represent the total number of calories you'll need (1200 to 1500 for women; 1800 to 2000 for men); see page 45 for recommended daily calorie counts. If you are a snacker, build up your calories with snacks from the list opposite. If you prefer to eat three times a day, like I do, add a smoothie of your choice to your breakfast (see pages 86–7), then build up your calories at lunch and dinner by adding a salad (see pages 134–5) or a little bit of extra carb (rice or pasta), or green or starchy veg and/or protein (see page 47 for portion sizes). Alternatively, just increase the portion size of the above meals.

Orange & Spinach Smoothie (page 89)	76/serve
Watercress & Cherry Smoothie (page 89)	99/serve
Avo Smash with Beetroot (page 236)	64/serve
Fresh Trail Mix (page 240)	40/serve
Green Goodness Soup (page 244)	133/serve
Cauliflower & Broccoli Popcorn (page 249)	59/serve
Sesame Cucumber Nuggets (page 257)	55/serve
Zucchini Hummus with Crackers (page 258)	324/serve
Almond Chai (page 277)	154/serve

*Serves 6; use leftovers for snack option

VEG & FRUIT
10 garlic cloves
7 cm ginger
10 spring onions
1 small red onion
2 small iceberg lettuce
100 g red cabbage
2 bunches kale
1 bunch silverbeet
2 bunches rainbow chard
4 witlof
2 bunches English spinach
1 bunch Chinese broccoli
1 bunch broccolini
1 Lebanese cucumber
6 zucchini
250 g fresh peas
750 g asparagus
750 g broccoli
200 g baby beans
100 g sweet potato
5 carrots
4 bunches baby carrots
4 bulbs baby fennel
250 g Brussels sprouts
1.65 kg cauliflower
350 g celeriac
250 g butternut pumpkin
500 g Kent pumpkin
2 avocadoes
4 kiwi fruit
6 bananas
2 peaches
1 large pineapple
5 lemons

FRESH HERBS
basil
bay leaves
dill
flat-leaf parsley
French tarragon
lemon thyme
thyme
2 long red chillies

BUTCHER
200 g beef fillet steak
800 g chicken thigh fillets,
  skin on
300 g skinless chicken breast
  fillets
300 g beef mince

FISHMONGER
100 g finely sliced raw
  sashimi-grade salmon
100 g raw prawn meat
12 peeled and deveined
  prawns
8 fresh whole sardines
600 g salmon fillet, skin and
  bones removed

DELI/OTHER
12 white anchovy fillets
130 g ready-made pesto
50 g soft goat's cheese
8 baby bocconcini
seasoned rice wine
  vinegar (sushi vinegar)
Sichuan pepper

+ KITCHEN STAPLES
(pages 58-9)

'Working up an
appetite with Paddy'

'♡ for LIFE xxx'

PART TWO

RECIPES *for* LIFE

'Yum!'

Breakfast

Purple Porridge . . . YUM!

BAKED PORRIDGE

SERVES 6 — PREP 15 MINUTES / STAND 20 MINUTES / COOK 55 MINUTES —
TOTAL CALORIES 858 / CALORIES PER SERVE 143

Make this delicious porridge the night before, or serve it as a dessert and use your leftovers for breakfast — it's so good. Just use a smidge of coconut or olive oil to grease the baking dish if you don't have cooking spray. And if you're all out of frozen berries, you can use chopped apple, pear or stone fruit.

1 tablespoon chia seeds

½ teaspoon vanilla bean paste or extract

1½ cups unsweetened almond milk

coconut oil or olive oil cooking spray

500 g frozen mixed berries

finely grated zest and juice of 1 orange

1 cup rolled oats

⅓ cup pumpkin seeds

½ teaspoon ground cinnamon

1 tablespoon pure maple syrup

1. Place the chia seeds in a bowl, add ⅓ cup cold water and stir well. Set aside for 15 minutes, stirring occasionally, or until the seeds are plump with a gel-like consistency. Add the vanilla and almond milk and whisk until well combined.

2. Meanwhile, preheat the oven to 180°C (160°C fan-forced). Lightly grease a 24 cm round baking dish with cooking spray.

3. Place the frozen berries and orange zest and juice in the prepared dish and mix well.

4. Add the oats, pumpkin seeds and cinnamon to the chia mixture and stir until well combined. Spoon the mixture over the berries and level the surface.

5. Bake for 50 minutes or until golden and set when tested in the centre with a skewer. Remove from the oven and immediately brush with the maple syrup.

6. Preheat a grill to high. Grill the porridge for 2 minutes or until the top is crisp and golden. Rest in the dish for 5 minutes before serving.

VEGAN VEGETARIAN

DAIRY FREE

REFINED SUGAR FREE

FREEZER FRIENDLY

BANANA PANCAKES *with* PINEAPPLE *and* STRAWBERRY SALSA

SERVES 4 — PREP 20 MINUTES / STAND 20 MINUTES / COOK 20 MINUTES —
TOTAL CALORIES 697 / CALORIES PER SERVE 174

These sweet little pancakes are great for anyone with a gluten intolerance.
Note that you must let the pancakes cook on their first side for the longer time of
4 minutes otherwise they will be too fragile to turn over (and you'll end up with
scrambled banana).

**300 g pineapple, skin and core
removed, finely chopped**

**250 g strawberries, hulled
and finely chopped**

2 teaspoons pure maple syrup

1 teaspoon lemon thyme leaves

2 large overripe bananas

4 eggs, whisked

coconut oil or olive oil cooking spray

1 Put the pineapple, strawberry, maple syrup and lemon thyme in
a bowl and gently stir to combine. Stand at room temperature for
20 minutes, stirring occasionally.

2 Peel the bananas and mash in a bowl until very smooth. Add the egg
and whisk together until well combined.

3 Heat a large non-stick frying pan over medium heat and spray lightly
with cooking spray. Drop 1 tablespoon measures of the banana mixture
into the pan to form rounds (you should have enough mixture to make
20 pancakes so you will have to do this in batches). Cook for 4 minutes,
then flip them over and cook for a further 1 minute or until golden and
cooked through. Keep warm while you make the remaining pancakes.

4 Stack five warm pancakes on each plate, with the fruit salsa spooned in
between and on top. Serve warm.

VEGETARIAN PALEO DAIRY FREE GLUTEN FREE REFINED SUGAR FREE LUNCHBOX FRIENDLY FREEZER FRIENDLY

What a great way to KICK OFF a Sunday! KIDS love pancakes.

ROSEWATER CITRUS *and* BERRIES
with YOGHURT

SERVES 4 — PREP 15 MINUTES / STAND 30 MINUTES — TOTAL CALORIES 721 / CALORIES PER SERVE 180

This dish is so divine I'm sure you'd get away with serving it as a dessert at a dinner party. To roast your pine nuts, pop them in a little pan over medium heat until they become golden, but don't take your eyes off them for one second or they'll burn. Larger supermarkets stock rosewater, or you can order it online.

125 g blueberries

125 g raspberries

250 g small strawberries, hulled and halved

2 oranges, peeled, sliced into rounds

1 ruby grapefruit, peeled, sliced into rounds

1 tablespoon honey

2 teaspoons rosewater

1 tablespoon pine nuts, roasted

⅓ cup full-cream Greek yoghurt

1 Place the berries, orange, grapefruit, honey and rosewater in a bowl and gently toss to combine. Stand, covered, at room temperature for 30 minutes or until the fruit starts to release its natural juices.

2 Divide the mixture among four bowls. Scatter with pine nuts and serve with the yoghurt.

VEGETARIAN   GLUTEN FREE   REFINED SUGAR FREE   LUNCHBOX FRIENDLY

Start your morning with some PASSION. ♡

COCONUT *and* PASSIONFRUIT CHIA PUDDINGS

SERVES 6 — PREP 20 MINUTES / STAND 10 MINUTES / CHILL 4 HOURS
TOTAL CALORIES 803 / CALORIES PER SERVE 134

If you've never tried fresh young coconuts, this is a great recipe to start you off. You'll need a chef's knife to cut an opening in the top (do it gradually so you don't lose any of the sweet juice). These puddings are perfect for dessert, too. Plus you can take the leftovers to work as a snack.

1 young coconut, top removed

3 passionfruit, halved, seeds and juice scraped

½ cup chia seeds

⅓ cup light coconut milk

1 tablespoon shredded coconut

1 Strain the coconut water from the coconut into a large jug, adding extra cold tap water (if needed) to reach a measurement of 400 ml. Use a spoon to scrape all the white flesh from the inside of the coconut. Transfer to a board and finely slice into strips. Put 2 tablespoons of the coconut strips in an airtight container in the fridge and reserve for later. Stir the remaining strips into the coconut water mixture.

2 Stir three-quarters of the passionfruit seeds and juice into the coconut water mixture. Store the remaining passionfruit seeds and juice in an airtight container in the fridge until you are ready to serve.

3 Using a fork, whisk the chia seeds into the coconut water mixture. Stand at room temperature for 10 minutes, then whisk again.

4 Pour the coconut milk into six 200 ml glasses or bowls. Spoon over the chia mixture, then chill for 4 hours or overnight if time permits.

5 Top the puddings with the shredded coconut, reserved coconut strips and reserved passionfruit seeds and juice. Serve cold.

VEGAN VEGETARIAN PALEO DAIRY FREE GLUTEN FREE REFINED SUGAR FREE LUNCHBOX FRIENDLY

EARL GREY *and* LEMON SYRUP MUFFIN BITES

MAKES 12 — PREP 15 MINUTES / STAND 20 MINUTES / COOK 15 MINUTES + COOLING —
TOTAL CALORIES 1414 / CALORIES PER SERVE 118

The ingredients in this little recipe are really easy to source (you'll probably
have most of them in your cupboard already). Store any leftovers in the fridge
and take them for lunch the next day.

1 earl grey teabag

1 cup boiling water

1 tablespoon chia seeds

⅓ cup extra light olive oil

1½ tablespoons pure maple syrup

coconut oil or olive oil cooking spray

2 tablespoons fresh lemon juice

1 cup self-raising wholemeal flour

**3 teaspoons finely grated
lemon zest**

1 tablespoon pumpkin seeds

1 Place the teabag in a large heatproof jug, pour in the boiling water
   and steep for 3 minutes. Discard the teabag and allow the tea mixture
   to cool to room temperature. Stir in the chia seeds and set aside for
   15 minutes or until the seeds are plump and gel like. Stir in the olive
   oil and 1 tablespoon maple syrup until well combined.

2 Meanwhile, preheat the oven to 180°C (160°C fan-forced) and lightly
   spray a 12-hole, 1 tablespoon capacity, rounded-base muffin tin with
   cooking spray. Combine the lemon juice and remaining maple syrup
   in a small jug.

3 Combine the flour and lemon zest in a bowl, add the tea mixture and
   stir until just combined – do not overmix or the muffins will be tough.
   Spoon the batter evenly into the prepared muffin holes and sprinkle
   the tops with pumpkin seeds.

4 Bake for 15 minutes or until golden and a skewer inserted in the centre
   comes out clean. Remove from the oven. Immediately pierce each
   muffin three times with the skewer, then liberally brush the juice and
   maple mixture over the hot muffins. Cool in the tin for 5 minutes.
   Serve warm or at room temperature.

VEGAN VEGETARIAN DAIRY FREE REFINED SUGAR FREE LUNCHBOX FRIENDLY FREEZER FRIENDLY

Watercress and Cherry 1

Kiwi and Avocado 2

Orange and Spinach 3

Peachy Cream 4

Blueberry and Banana 5

Tahini and Mango 6

Ultra Chocolate 7

Tropical Kale 8

Smoothies
FOR TWO

EACH RECIPE MAKES 400–500 ML

Adding frozen fruit to smoothies not only makes them lovely and cold
but gives a wonderfully thick and creamy texture.

1 WATERCRESS + CHERRY

1 cup watercress leaves
1 cup frozen pitted cherries
1 chopped tomato
3 cm piece of ginger, chopped
½ cup coconut water

TOTAL CALORIES 197
CALORIES PER SERVE 99

2 KIWI + AVOCADO

1 chopped kiwi fruit
¼ avocado
½ cup flat-leaf parsley leaves
1 tablespoon full-cream
  cottage cheese
1 chopped frozen banana
½ teaspoon ground cinnamon
½ cup unsweetened almond milk

TOTAL CALORIES 289
CALORIES PER SERVE 145

3 ORANGE + SPINACH

2 chopped oranges
2 cups baby spinach leaves
1 cup mint leaves
½ teaspoon ground turmeric
½ cup water

TOTAL CALORIES 152
CALORIES PER SERVE 76

4 PEACHY CREAM

1 chopped peach
1 cup frozen chopped pineapple
3 tablespoons raw macadamias
½ cup coconut milk

TOTAL CALORIES 459
CALORIES PER SERVE 230

5 BLUEBERRY + BANANA

250 g frozen blueberries
1 chopped frozen banana
½ cup rice milk
1 egg

TOTAL CALORIES 356
CALORIES PER SERVE 178

6 TAHINI + MANGO

2 teaspoons tahini
1 cup chopped frozen mango
½ teaspoon vanilla bean paste
  or extract
¾ cup water

TOTAL CALORIES 229
CALORIES PER SERVE 115

7 ULTRA CHOCOLATE

1 tablespoon raw cacao powder
  (see page 296)
1 chopped frozen banana
100 g silken tofu
2 tablespoons pure maple syrup
½ cup unsweetened
  almond milk

TOTAL CALORIES 331
CALORIES PER SERVE 166

8 TROPICAL KALE

2 kale leaves
1 cup chopped frozen papaya
seeds and pulp of 4 passionfruit
½ cup coconut water

TOTAL CALORIES 140
CALORIES PER SERVE 70

GLUTEN-FREE BIRCHER BOWLS

SERVES 4 — PREP 15 MINUTES + COOLING / COOK 10 MINUTES / CHILL 6 HOURS —
TOTAL CALORIES 1117 / CALORIES PER SERVE 279

Bircher is basically muesli that needs a bit of soaking or cooking, and this one tastes so much better if you can get it ready the night before. It's extra nutritious because I use quinoa flakes (they're in the health-food aisle at the supermarket). When it's time to serve your bircher, warm the jar of honey first (sit it in a dish of boiled water or microwave it on high for 20 seconds), so that you can pour exactly 2 teaspoons and not blow your calorie quota. Or better still, don't use any honey at all – the apple and grapes should be sweet enough.

1 cup quinoa flakes

1 cup rice milk

1 green apple, coarsely grated

½ teaspoon mixed spice

3 tablespoons Labne (see page 333)

8 seedless red grapes, sliced crossways

8 seedless green grapes, sliced crossways

3 tablespoons slivered almonds, roasted

2 teaspoons honey, warmed

1 Place the quinoa flakes and 1 cup water in a saucepan over medium heat. Bring to a simmer and cook, stirring occasionally, for 10 minutes. Transfer to a heatproof bowl and cool to room temperature.

2 Add the rice milk, apple and mixed spice to the quinoa mixture and stir until well combined. Cover with plastic film and chill for at least 6 hours or until the bircher has thickened slightly.

3 Divide the bircher among four bowls. Top with labne, grapes and almonds and finish with a drizzle of honey.

VEGETARIAN GLUTEN FREE REFINED SUGAR FREE

STRAWBERRY CHIA JAM

MAKES 3 CUPS {36 SERVES/1 TABLESPOON PER SERVE} — PREP 10 MINUTES / COOK 10 MINUTES + COOLING /
STAND 15 MINUTES — TOTAL CALORIES 282 / CALORIES PER SERVE 8

This simple little recipe is a great example of how healthy eating doesn't mean
you have to deprive yourself. The strawberries and lemon juice give you a stack
of vitamin C, the chia seeds a little fibre and protein, and yet you are eating *jam*!
This is delicious served with Spiced Sweet Pumpkin Scones (see page 307).

**500 g strawberries,
hulled and chopped**

2 tablespoons pure maple syrup

1 tablespoon fresh lemon juice

1 tablespoon chia seeds

1 Place the strawberries, syrup and lemon juice in a saucepan over
medium heat. Bring to a simmer, then reduce the heat to low and
simmer gently, stirring occasionally, for 10 minutes or until the
strawberries collapse and release their juices.

2 Transfer the strawberry mixture to a heatproof bowl and allow to
cool to room temperature.

3 Stir in the chia seeds. Set aside for 15 minutes, stirring occasionally,
until the seeds are plump and have a gel-like consistency. Use the
jam straight away or store in an airtight container in the fridge for
up to 1 week.

VEGAN
VEGETARIAN   PALEO   DAIRY
FREE   GLUTEN
FREE   REFINED
SUGAR FREE   LUNCHBOX
FRIENDLY

I sometimes grab a handful of this for a SNACK TO GO.

NO-BAKE GRANOLA

SERVES 10 (½ CUP PER SERVE) — PREP 5 MINUTES — TOTAL CALORIES 1725 / CALORIES PER SERVE 173

Granola, muesli – whatever you call it, this is one nutritious, family-friendly breakfast cereal. Double the quantities and you've got brekkie sorted for a good while. Serve with whatever milk you prefer (I have mine with water). Adding ½ cup unsweetened almond milk adds an extra 15 calories per serve. Freeze-dried strawberries are available from health-food shops, or you can buy them online.

1 cup rolled oats

2 cups puffed rice

½ cup mixed seeds (sunflower seeds, pumpkin seeds, linseeds)

½ cup mixed raw unsalted nuts (pecans, walnuts, almonds, cashews, brazil nuts, hazelnuts), chopped

½ cup craisins

⅔ cup freeze-dried strawberries

1 Place all the ingredients into a large bowl and mix until well combined. Store in an airtight container at room temperature for up to 1 month.

VEGAN VEGETARIAN   DAIRY FREE   GLUTEN FREE   REFINED SUGAR FREE   LUNCHBOX FRIENDLY

BANANA MAPLE FRENCH TOAST

SERVES 4 — PREP 15 MINUTES / COOK 15 MINUTES — TOTAL CALORIES 1238 / CALORIES PER SERVE 310

It might look plain and simple, but this brekkie is absolutely delicious.
It's pretty high in calories, so either have it on days when you know you're going
to train, or halve your serving size. Active teenagers can hoe in.

1 large ripe banana

2 teaspoons pure maple syrup

345 g rye sourdough loaf,
cut into 16 × 1 cm thick slices

2 eggs, whisked

coconut oil or olive oil cooking spray

½ teaspoon pure icing sugar

1 Mash the banana and maple syrup together, then spread evenly over one side of half the sourdough slices. Sandwich together with the remaining slices.

2 Whisk the egg and 2 tablespoons water in a shallow bowl. Dip the banana sandwiches into the egg mixture, making sure they are coated on all sides.

3 Heat a large non-stick frying pan over medium heat and spray lightly with cooking spray. Add half the sandwiches and cook for 3 minutes each side or until golden. Remove and dust lightly with icing sugar. Repeat with the remaining sandwiches and serve warm.

VEGETARIAN   DAIRY FREE

Hello. I die. SHUT UP.

This one's a WINNER with my next-door neighbour!

RASPBERRY, COCONUT *and* DARK CHOC LOAF

SERVES 10   PREP 15 MINUTES / COOK 50 MINUTES / STAND 20 MINUTES —
TOTAL CALORIES 1900 / CALORIES PER SERVE 190

This loaf is delicious when served slightly warm, but it is very fragile when first baked so it's important to let it rest in the tin for 20 minutes before slicing. Store the loaf in an airtight container in the fridge for up to 5 days and toast before serving. Unsweetened apple puree is available from larger supermarkets, health-food shops and online.

½ cup coconut flour

1 cup arrowroot (tapioca flour)

1 cup desiccated coconut

1 teaspoon bicarbonate of soda

1½ cups frozen raspberries

1 cup unsweetened apple puree

1 tablespoon vanilla bean paste or extract

4 eggs, whisked

50 g dark chocolate (80 per cent cocoa), broken into pieces

1   Preheat the oven to 180°C (160°C fan-forced). Line the base and sides of an 18 cm × 9 cm loaf tin with baking paper.

2   Mix together the coconut flour, arrowroot, coconut, bicarbonate of soda and 1 cup raspberries in a bowl. Whisk the apple puree, vanilla and egg until well combined. Add to the dry ingredients and stir until just combined, then immediately spoon into the prepared tin. Level the surface. Scatter over the remaining raspberries and gently press into the batter, then press in the chocolate.

3   Bake for 50 minutes or until golden and a skewer inserted in the centre comes out clean. Rest in the tin for 20 minutes, then transfer to a wire rack to cool. Cut into 10 slices and serve.

VEGETARIAN   PALEO   GLUTEN FREE   REFINED SUGAR FREE   LUNCHBOX FRIENDLY   FREEZER FRIENDLY

ZUCCHINI, HAM *and* CHEDDAR MUFFINS

MAKES 12 — PREP 25 MINUTES / COOK 35 MINUTES + COOLING —
TOTAL CALORIES 1445 / CALORIES PER SERVE 120

A perfect combo of complex carbs, protein and fats for sustained energy.
Make up a double batch and freeze half. They'll keep in an airtight container
in the fridge for 3 days or individually wrapped in the freezer (use little
zip-lock bags) for up to 3 months.

1 large zucchini

1 carrot, coarsely grated

50 g shaved ham, finely chopped

1 cup self-raising wholemeal flour

1 teaspoon baking powder

**3 tablespoons grated
vintage cheddar**

2 eggs, whisked

⅓ cup light olive oil

**3 tablespoons unsweetened
almond milk**

1   Preheat the oven to 180°C (160°C fan-forced). Line a 12-hole, ⅓-cup capacity muffin tin with paper patty cases.

2   Very finely slice 24 rounds from the zucchini and set aside. Coarsely grate the remaining zucchini and place in a large bowl with the carrot, ham, flour, baking powder and 2 tablespoons of the cheddar. Season to taste and stir until well combined.

3   Whisk the egg, oil and almond milk together in a jug. Pour into the dry ingredients and stir gently until just combined.

4   Spoon the mixture into the prepared paper cases and top with the zucchini rounds and remaining cheddar. Season to taste.

5   Bake for 35 minutes or until golden and a skewer inserted in the centre comes out clean. Cool in the tin for 5 minutes then serve warm or transfer to a wire rack to cool.

REFINED   LUNCHBOX   FREEZER
SUGAR FREE   FRIENDLY   FRIENDLY

Honing my SKILLS ready
for Axel's lunchbox!

MINTED MELON *with* FETA *and* PANCETTA

SERVES 4 — PREP 20 MINUTES / COOK 2 MINUTES + COOLING — TOTAL CALORIES 790 / CALORIES PER SERVE 198

So quick to make and such amazing colours and clean flavours. This is another
gorgeous breakfast that's high in antioxidants and will have your tastebuds zinging.

**500 g honeydew melon, peeled,
seeded and chopped**

**500 g watermelon, peeled
and chopped**

1 grapefruit, peeled and segmented

**1 ruby grapefruit, peeled
and segmented**

⅓ cup small mint leaves

2 thin slices hot pancetta

100 g Danish feta, crumbled

1 Place the melon, grapefruit and mint in a bowl and stir gently to
   combine. Set aside.

2 Preheat a grill to high. Cook the pancetta under the grill for 1 minute
   each side or until very crisp and golden. Cool to room temperature,
   then break into pieces.

3 Divide the melon mixture among four plates. Sprinkle with feta and
   pancetta and serve.

GLUTEN
FREE

REFINED
SUGAR FREE

LUNCHBOX
FRIENDLY

I had my first taste of cornbread
at Sylvia's Restaurant in HARLEM.
GREAT SOULFOOD.

VEGETABLE CORNBREAD

SERVES 12 — PREP 15 MINUTES / COOK 40 MINUTES / STAND 5 MINUTES —
TOTAL CALORIES 1797 / CALORIES PER SERVE 150

Polenta is made from ground corn kernels (cornmeal) and adds a nice crumbly
texture to baked goods. This nutritious bread is lovely for breakfast, but also makes
an excellent snack. Store in an airtight container in the fridge for up to 3 days or
freeze individually wrapped slices for up to 3 months.

1 cup polenta

1 cup self-raising wholemeal flour

1 corn cob, kernels removed

**1 green capsicum, seeded
and finely chopped**

1 carrot, coarsely grated

1 cup buttermilk

2 eggs, whisked

1 tablespoon honey

25 g butter, melted and cooled

1 long red chilli, finely chopped

1 Preheat the oven to 180°C (160°C fan-forced). Line the base and sides
   of a 20 cm square cake tin with baking paper.

2 Place the polenta, flour, corn, capsicum and carrot in a bowl and mix
   together well. Season to taste.

3 Whisk together the buttermilk, egg, honey and butter in a large jug.
   Add to the dry ingredients and mix until just combined. Spoon the
   batter into the prepared tin and level the surface. Sprinkle the chilli
   over the top.

4 Bake for 40 minutes or until golden and a skewer inserted in the centre
   comes out clean. Rest in the tin for 5 minutes, then cut into slices and
   serve warm.

VEGETARIAN   REFINED
              SUGAR FREE   LUNCHBOX
                           FRIENDLY   FREEZER
                                      FRIENDLY

BAKED RATATOUILLE EGGS

SERVES 4 — PREP 20 MINUTES / COOK 25 MINUTES — TOTAL CALORIES 611 / CALORIES PER SERVE 153

Could you fit any more fresh veggies in a breakfast dish? I think not. This is so nutritious and low in calories I'd serve it for dinner. If you're feeding large or growing humans, serve it with a slice of Vegetable Cornbread (see page 101) or some wholemeal toast.

2 spring onions, sliced

2 baby eggplants, sliced

125 g cherry tomatoes, halved

2 celery stalks, chopped

2 zucchini, chopped

1 red capsicum, seeded and chopped

1 tablespoon tomato paste with herbs

1 cup Vegetable Stock (see page 331)

⅓ cup small basil leaves, chopped, plus 1 tablespoon extra, to serve

4 eggs

2 teaspoons finely grated parmesan

1 Preheat the oven to 180°C (160°C fan-forced). Place four 2-cup capacity ovenproof bowls on a baking tray.

2 Combine the onion, eggplant, tomato, celery, zucchini, capsicum, tomato paste and stock in a large saucepan over high heat. Bring to the boil, stirring, then reduce the heat to low and cook, covered and stirring occasionally, for 10 minutes or until the vegetables are soft. Remove the pan from the heat, add the basil and season to taste. Stir until well combined.

3 Spoon the vegetable mixture evenly into the bowls. Using the back of a large spoon, make an indent in the centre of each bowl, then carefully crack an egg into each indent, taking care not to break the yolk.

4 Bake for 15 minutes or until the egg whites have set and the yolks are still runny. Sprinkle with parmesan and extra basil leaves, and serve warm.

VEGETARIAN   GLUTEN FREE   REFINED SUGAR FREE   FREEZER FRIENDLY

CURRIED GREENS *and* OMELETTE RIBBONS

SERVES 4 — PREP 15 MINUTES / COOK 10 MINUTES — TOTAL CALORIES 344 / CALORIES PER SERVE 86

For a more substantial meal, add ½ cup leftover cooked brown basmati rice to
the curry paste when cooking (this will add another 94 calories per serve).

2 eggs

2 tablespoons chopped chives

coconut oil or olive oil cooking spray

2 teaspoons korma curry paste

**100 g green beans, trimmed,
finely sliced on the diagonal**

**200 g broccoli, chopped
(including stem)**

**1 bunch silverbeet, stalks removed,
leaves finely shredded**

1 lemon, cut into wedges

1 Whisk the eggs, chives and 2 tablespoons water in a jug.
Season to taste.

2 Preheat a 20 cm non-stick frying pan over medium–high heat and
spray lightly with cooking spray. Pour half the egg mixture into the pan,
tilting to form a thin omelette over the base. Cook for 1 minute or until
the egg is cooked and light golden. Transfer the omelette to a piece of
baking paper. Repeat with the remaining egg mixture to make a second
thin omelette. Cool to room temperature, then roll each omelette up
and thinly slice. Set aside.

3 Meanwhile, heat a deep frying pan over high heat. Add the curry paste
and cook, stirring, for 1 minute or until fragrant. Add the beans and
broccoli and cook, stirring occasionally, for 3 minutes. Finally, add the
silverbeet and ½ cup water and cook, tossing, for 1 minute or until the
silverbeet is just starting to wilt. Season to taste.

4 Divide the silverbeet mixture among four plates. Top with the omelette
ribbons and serve with lemon wedges.

VEGETARIAN   PALEO   DAIRY
FREE   GLUTEN
FREE   REFINED
SUGAR FREE   LUNCHBOX
FRIENDLY

I love MEDITERRANEAN eating.
This is one of my FAVES.

MEDITERRANEAN BEANS

SERVES 4 — PREP 15 MINUTES / STAND 1 HOUR / COOK 10 MINUTES —
TOTAL CALORIES 699 / CALORIES PER SERVE 175

These beans are even more delicious if you cover and chill them overnight
in the fridge. Just bring them to room temperature again before serving.
Serve with a poached egg for an additional 71 calories per serve.

**1 × 400 g tin cannellini beans,
drained and rinsed**

**1 quantity Nutty Herb Dressing
(see page 146)**

8 yellow squash, halved horizontally

**2 red capsicums, cut into rings,
seeds removed**

50 g baby rocket leaves

1 Place the beans in a bowl and pour over the dressing. Stand, covered, at room temperature for at least 1 hour.

2 Heat a large chargrill pan over high heat. Add the squash and capsicum separately and chargrill for 5 minutes each or until just tender and golden. Transfer to a heatproof bowl and cool slightly.

3 Add the bean mixture and rocket to the vegetables, season to taste and toss gently to combine. Divide among four plates and serve.

VEGAN VEGETARIAN   PALEO   DAIRY FREE   GLUTEN FREE   REFINED SUGAR FREE   LUNCHBOX FRIENDLY

What's not to LOVE?

PUMPKIN *and* CELERIAC ROSTI

SERVES 4 — PREP 20 MINUTES / COOK 40 MINUTES / STAND 5 MINUTES —
TOTAL CALORIES 430 / CALORIES PER SERVE 108

This delicious rosti is dead easy. I love how the crisp celeriac and sweet pumpkin
flavours balance each other so perfectly. Cook it in one heavy-based ovenproof pan
or four little ones. White anchovies are different from the regular brown ones.
Ask your local deli for them, or look online – they're worth the effort.

**250 g pumpkin, peeled, seeded
and coarsely grated**

**350 g celeriac, peeled
and coarsely grated**

**2 tablespoons dill fronds,
plus extra to serve**

1 egg

1 tablespoon coconut flour

coconut oil or olive oil cooking spray

**⅓ cup Fermented Slaw
(see page 332)**

12 white anchovy fillets

3 tablespoons Labne (see page 333)

1 Preheat the oven to 220°C (200°C fan-forced).

2 Combine the pumpkin, celeriac, dill, egg and coconut flour in a bowl
and season to taste.

3 Spray a large (30 cm) ovenproof heavy-based frying pan with cooking
spray. Press the vegetable mixture over the base and side of the pan
as firmly as possible and lightly spray the top with cooking spray.

4 Place the pan in the oven and bake for 40 minutes or until cooked,
crisp and golden. Rest in the pan for 5 minutes, then cut into four
portions and serve topped with fermented slaw, anchovies, labne
and a scattering of dill.

GLUTEN
FREE

REFINED
SUGAR FREE

GARLIC MUSHROOMS *and* DUKKAH AVOCADO

SERVES 4 — PREP 15 MINUTES / COOK 10 MINUTES — TOTAL CALORIES 478 / CALORIES PER SERVE 120

Mushroom and avocado are made for each other, and when you add the chilli, lime and dukkah the flavour is just awesome. But it's the watercress that gives this dish its five-star health rating – watercress is officially the most nutrient-dense veggie on Earth. Dukkah is a North African nut, seed and spice mix. You'll find it in the spice aisle of larger supermarkets.

extra virgin olive oil cooking spray

4 large field mushrooms, stalks removed and finely sliced

2 garlic cloves, finely sliced

1 long green chilli, seeded and finely sliced

1 lime, cut into wedges

1 small avocado, halved, then each half cut lengthways into 4 wedges

2 tablespoons dukkah

2 cups watercress leaves

1 Preheat the oven to 220°C (200°C fan-forced) and line a large baking tray with baking paper.

2 Lightly spray both sides of the mushrooms with cooking spray. Place on the prepared tray, cup-side up, then fill the cups with the sliced stalk, garlic and chilli. Season to taste, then lightly spray with cooking spray.

3 Bake for 10 minutes or until the mushrooms are starting to soften, but don't let them collapse.

4 Meanwhile, squeeze two of the lime wedges over the avocado, then dip one side of each avocado wedge in dukkah. Set aside.

5 Top each mushroom with two wedges of dukkah avocado. Add watercress, then serve warm with the remaining lime wedges.

VEGAN VEGETARIAN   PALEO   DAIRY FREE   GLUTEN FREE   REFINED SUGAR FREE

I never used to eat a lot of AVOCADO, but since being with Steve I enjoy more HEALTHY FATS.

BEETS for BREKKIE!

SUMAC ROASTED BEETS *and* TOMATOES *with* FRIED EGG

SERVES 4   PREP 15 MINUTES / COOK 25 MINUTES — TOTAL CALORIES 532 / CALORIES PER SERVE 133

Sumac is a Middle Eastern spice with a tangy lemon flavour. It should be pretty easy to find in the spice aisle at a big supermarket. If you can't get hold of sumac, combine lemon zest with a pinch of salt, although it won't have quite the same exotic flavour.

4 baby beetroot, trimmed, skins scrubbed, cut into thin wedges

4 roma tomatoes, quartered lengthways

250 g cherry tomatoes

2 teaspoons ground sumac

1 teaspoon extra virgin olive oil

extra virgin olive oil cooking spray

4 eggs

flat-leaf parsley leaves, to garnish

1 Preheat the oven to 220°C (200°C fan-forced). Line a large baking tray with baking paper.

2 Place the beetroot, tomatoes, sumac and olive oil in a bowl. Season to taste and toss to combine. Spread the mixture evenly over the prepared tray and bake for 20 minutes or until just tender and golden.

3 Heat a large non-stick frying pan over medium heat. Spray lightly with cooking spray, then crack the eggs into the pan and cook for 2 minutes or until the egg whites have set but the yolks are still runny.

4 Divide the tomato mixture among serving plates and sprinkle with parsley. Top each portion with an egg and serve warm.

VEGETARIAN PALEO DAIRY FREE GLUTEN FREE REFINED SUGAR FREE

VEGETABLE BAKED BEANS

SERVES 4 — PREP 15 MINUTES / COOK 35 MINUTES —
TOTAL CALORIES 1184 / CALORIES PER SERVE 296

Jam-packed with veggies, these guys will get you moving . . .

1 onion, finely chopped

1 carrot, finely chopped

2 celery stalks, finely chopped

1 zucchini, finely chopped

**1 red capsicum, seeded
and finely chopped**

2 teaspoons smoked paprika

**2 cups Tomato Passata
(see page 330)**

2 small rosemary sprigs

**2 × 400 g tins red kidney beans,
drained and rinsed**

1 Preheat the oven to 200°C (180°C fan-forced).

2 Place the onion, carrot, celery, zucchini, capsicum and paprika in a deep flameproof casserole dish over high heat and cook, stirring, for 1 minute. Add ½ cup water and stir, then reduce the heat to low. Cover and simmer gently, stirring occasionally, for 10 minutes or until the vegetables are soft and the liquid has reduced.

3 Add the passata, rosemary and beans to the dish and stir until the mixture comes to the boil. Season to taste.

4 Cover and transfer to the oven. Bake for 20 minutes or until the mixture has reduced and thickened. Serve warm.

| VEGAN VEGETARIAN | DAIRY FREE | GLUTEN FREE | REFINED SUGAR FREE | FREEZER FRIENDLY |

DILL-PICKLED MUSHROOMS
and GLAZED SPROUTS

SERVES 4 — PREP 20 MINUTES / STAND 1 HOUR / COOK 10 MINUTES —
TOTAL CALORIES 1038 / CALORIES PER SERVE 260

Steve loves pickles and mushrooms, so this one's a winner!

300 g button mushrooms, finely sliced

1 quantity Lemon Vinaigrette (see page 146)

3 tablespoons dill fronds

20 g butter

200 g small Brussels sprouts, trimmed and halved

½ cup walnut halves

2 teaspoons honey

1 bunch kale, stalks removed, leaves torn

1 Place the sliced mushrooms, vinaigrette and dill in a bowl and season to taste. Cover and leave to marinate at room temperature for 1 hour.

2 Melt the butter in a large, deep frying pan over medium–high heat. Add the sprouts, walnuts and honey and cook, stirring occasionally, for 5 minutes or until the walnuts turn golden. Add the kale and 2 tablespoons water. Cook, tossing, for 2 minutes or until the kale just wilts and the sprouts are just tender.

3 Divide the sprout mixture among four plates. Top with the marinated mushrooms and serve warm.

VEGETARIAN   PALEO   GLUTEN FREE   REFINED SUGAR FREE

MULTI-PURPOSE
Frittata

SERVES 6 — PREP 10 MINUTES / COOK 45 MINUTES — TOTAL CALORIES 714 / CALORIES PER SERVE 119

Eat these versatile goodies for breakfast, lunch or dinner, at home or on the go,
or enjoy the mini muffin size as a snack. If you don't have an ovenproof frying pan,
cook the frittata in a 28 cm x 18 cm baking tin or a 22 cm round cake tin –
just make sure you line the tin with baking paper first.

coconut oil or olive oil cooking spray

1 zucchini, coarsely grated

6 eggs, whisked

250 g full-cream cottage cheese

2 spring onions, finely sliced

3 tablespoons small basil leaves

1 Preheat the oven to 200°C (180°C fan-forced).
Spray a 22 cm heavy-based ovenproof frying pan
with cooking spray.

2 Place the zucchini, egg, cottage cheese and
spring onion in a bowl and stir until well
combined. Season to taste.

3 Pour the mixture into the prepared pan and bake
for 45 minutes or until golden and cooked when
tested in the centre with a knife. Cool in the pan
for 2 minutes. Sprinkle with basil and season to
taste, then cut into slices and serve warm.

4 Store leftovers in an airtight container in the
fridge for up to 3 days or freeze individual
portions for up to 2 months.

Individual frittatas: Spoon the mixture into
a 12-hole, ⅓ cup-capacity muffin tin lined with
paper patty cases and bake for 30 minutes.

Mini frittatas: Spoon the mixture into two 24-hole
mini muffin tins lined with paper patty cases and
bake for 20 minutes.

VARIATIONS: ADD TO THE BASIC RECIPE AND BAKE

SWEET POTATO AND SALMON
2 teaspoons smoked paprika
100 g coarsely grated sweet potato
1 x 210 g tin red salmon, drained and flaked
TOTAL CALORIES 964/ CALORIES PER SERVE 161

SPRING VEGETABLE
½ cup fresh peas
1 bunch asparagus, trimmed and cut into 3 cm lengths
½ cup small broccoli florets
2 teaspoons finely grated lemon zest
TOTAL CALORIES 806/ CALORIES PER SERVE 135

ROAST PUMPKIN AND BLACK BEAN
200 g dry-roasted chopped pumpkin
1 x 400 g tin black beans, rinsed
TOTAL CALORIES 1034/ CALORIES PER SERVE 172

SPECK AND TOMATO
50 g finely chopped speck
⅓ cup semi-dried tomato strips in brine, finely chopped
50 g Danish feta, crumbled
TOTAL CALORIES 1177/ CALORIES PER SERVE 196

ANTIPASTO CHICKEN
100 g chopped cooked chicken
½ cup antipasto vegetables in brine, chopped
TOTAL CALORIES 979/ CALORIES PER SERVE 163

These are great the NEXT DAY,
or the day after . . .

CAULIFLOWER *and* PEA FRITTERS
with HALOUMI

SERVES 4 — PREP 15 MINUTES / COOK 20 MINUTES — TOTAL CALORIES 516 / CALORIES PER SERVE 129

Haloumi, a firm, white salty cheese made from goat's or sheep's milk, is just perfect with the naturally sweet cauliflower and baby peas in this recipe. The fritters might look a bit crumbly at first when placed in the pan but as they cook on the first side the haloumi will melt and bind the mixture together more firmly.

200 g cauliflower, trimmed and finely chopped

1 cup frozen baby peas, thawed

2 eggs, whisked

2 tablespoons self-raising wholemeal flour

50 g haloumi, finely chopped

coconut oil or olive oil cooking spray

125 g cherry tomatoes, halved

50 g baby spinach leaves

1 Place the cauliflower, peas, egg, flour and haloumi in a bowl. Season to taste and mix until well combined.

2 Heat a large frying pan over low heat and spray lightly with cooking spray. For each fritter spoon 3 tablespoons of mixture into the pan and press firmly into rounds. Depending on the size of your pan you will probably need to do this in two batches of four (to make eight fritters in total). Cook for 5 minutes, then carefully flip the fritters over and cook the other side for 4 minutes or until golden and cooked through.

3 Put two fritters on each plate, along with the cherry tomatoes and baby spinach, and serve warm.

VEGETARIAN   REFINED SUGAR FREE   LUNCHBOX FRIENDLY   FREEZER FRIENDLY

YOGHURT FLATBREADS

MAKES 12 — PREP 20 MINUTES / STAND 20 MINUTES / COOK 10 MINUTES —
TOTAL CALORIES 735 / CALORIES PER SERVE 61

I've always wanted to make my own healthy version of flatbread and this one is a beauty.
If you find the dough too sticky to handle just add another 1–2 tablespoons of flour.
Likewise, if the dough feels too dry add 1–2 tablespoons of yoghurt. For variation,
try using cumin seeds, crushed coriander seeds, fennel seeds or mustard seeds in
place of the sesame seeds.

¾ cup self-raising wholemeal flour

½ teaspoon baking powder

1½ teaspoons sea salt flakes

½ cup full-cream Greek yoghurt

1 tablespoon sesame seeds

extra virgin olive oil cooking spray

**1 cup Tomato Passata
(see page 330)**

1 Place the flour, baking powder and 1 teaspoon salt in a bowl and stir until well combined. Add the yoghurt and stir until almost combined, then use your hands to bring the dough together. Knead lightly until a smooth ball forms, then cover with a tea towel and leave to stand at room temperature for 20 minutes.

2 Form 1 tablespoon measures of the dough into balls, then roll out each ball between sheets of baking paper to a 10 cm round with a thickness of about 2 mm. Sprinkle the tops with sesame seeds and lightly roll over to press the seeds into the dough.

3 Heat a large chargrill pan over medium heat. Lightly spray each side of the dough rounds with cooking spray and chargrill, in batches, for 1 minute each side or until golden and cooked through. Serve warm or at room temperature with passata for dipping.

VEGETARIAN   REFINED SUGAR FREE   LUNCHBOX FRIENDLY FREEZER FRIENDLY

Start your day with
the POWER of GREEN.

BREAKFAST GREENS *with* SPICED CHICKPEAS

SERVES 4 — PREP 15 MINUTES / COOK 10 MINUTES — TOTAL CALORIES 728 / CALORIES PER SERVE 182

This is a health retreat on a plate! You've got your leafy greens with all their vitamins, minerals and fibre, your chickpeas with their protein (and more fibre), and your antioxidant flavour hits from the turmeric, lime and coriander. It also makes a super-quick evening meal.

1 tablespoon coconut oil

1 × 400 g tin chickpeas, drained and rinsed

½ teaspoon cayenne pepper

1 teaspoon ground turmeric

1 baby bok choy, leaves separated

200 g green cabbage, thinly shredded

1 bunch English spinach, leaves torn

½ cup Vegetable Stock (see page 331)

⅓ cup small coriander sprigs

1 small lime, cut into wedges

1 Heat half the coconut oil in a wok over high heat. Once melted, add the chickpeas, cayenne and turmeric and cook, tossing, for 3 minutes or until crisp and golden. Transfer the chickpeas to a heatproof bowl and cover to keep warm.

2 Heat the remaining oil in the same wok over high heat. Once melted, add the bok choy, cabbage, spinach and stock and cook, tossing, for 2 minutes or until the bok choy stems and cabbage are just tender and the spinach leaves have started to wilt.

3 Divide the vegetable mixture among four bowls, season to taste and top with the spiced chickpeas and coriander sprigs. Serve warm, with lime wedges.

VEGAN VEGETARIAN   DAIRY FREE   GLUTEN FREE   REFINED SUGAR FREE

SPINACH *and* FENNEL PIKELETS *with* BACON

SERVES 4 — PREP 20 MINUTES / COOK 20 MINUTES — TOTAL CALORIES 954 / CALORIES PER SERVE 239

A veggie-laden healthy twist on pikelets.

coconut oil or olive oil cooking spray

1 rindless bacon rasher,
finely chopped

1 small red onion, finely chopped

1 baby fennel bulb, trimmed and
finely chopped, fronds reserved

20 g baby spinach leaves,
finely shredded

4 eggs, whisked

½ cup almond meal

½ cup arrowroot (tapioca flour)

2 tablespoons pure maple syrup

1   Heat a large frying pan over medium heat and lightly spray with cooking spray. Add the bacon and cook, stirring occasionally, for 5 minutes or until crisp and golden. Using a slotted spoon, transfer to a plate lined with paper towel.

2   Meanwhile, place the onion, fennel, spinach, egg, almond meal and arrowroot in a bowl. Season to taste and stir until well combined.

3   Reheat the same frying pan over medium heat and lightly spray again with cooking spray. Working in batches, pour 3 tablespoon measures of the mixture into rounds in the pan and cook for 2 minutes each side or until cooked through and golden. Remove and keep warm while you make the remaining pikelets – you should have enough mixture to make 12 in total.

4   Divide the pikelets among serving plates. Top with the bacon and reserved fennel fronds and serve warm, drizzled with maple syrup.

PALEO	DAIRY FREE	GLUTEN FREE	REFINED SUGAR FREE	FREEZER FRIENDLY

HARISSA SPINACH *and* LENTILS

SERVES 4 — PREP 15 MINUTES / COOK 10 MINUTES — TOTAL CALORIES 900 / CALORIES PER SERVE 225

Harissa is a spicy North African paste made from red chilli, paprika, garlic and olive oil.
It is available in the spice aisle of large supermarkets.

1 red onion, cut into thin wedges

4 cap mushrooms, thickly sliced

1 teaspoon harissa paste

2 bunches English spinach, trimmed, stalks chopped, leaves torn

1 × 400 g tin lentils, drained and rinsed

8 baby roma tomatoes, halved lengthways

½ cup Vegetable Stock (see page 331)

4 soft-boiled eggs (see page 264), peeled and halved

½ cup chopped herbs (flat-leaf parsley, mint and/or coriander)

1 Place the onion, mushroom, harissa, spinach, lentils, tomato and stock in a large saucepan over high heat. Bring to the boil, then reduce the heat to low and simmer gently, covered and stirring occasionally, for 10 minutes or until the vegetables are just tender.

2 Divide the spinach mixture among four bowls. Top each with a soft-boiled egg and a scattering of herbs and serve warm.

VEGETARIAN   DAIRY FREE   GLUTEN FREE   REFINED SUGAR FREE

Lunch

HEARTY CHICKEN *and* RISONI SOUP

SERVES 4 — PREP 15 MINUTES / COOK 20 MINUTES / STAND 3 MINUTES —
TOTAL CALORIES 973 / CALORIES PER SERVE 243

This one ticks all my boxes: it's easy to make, not too heavy on the calories and has
a really good balance of macronutrients (carbs, proteins and fats). Risoni, also called
orzo, is rice-shaped pasta. It's perfect for hearty soups like this one.

**1.5 litres Chicken Stock
(see page 331)**

2 chicken thigh fillets, skin removed

1 leek, finely sliced and washed

2 tablespoons thyme leaves

2 zucchini, finely sliced

½ cup risoni

50 g baby spinach leaves

½ cup frozen baby peas

1 cup basil leaves, torn

1 Place the stock, chicken and leek in a large saucepan over high heat.
Bring to the boil, then reduce the heat to medium and simmer, covered,
for 15 minutes or until the chicken is cooked. Transfer the chicken to
a heatproof board and finely chop.

2 Return the chicken to the pan, add the thyme, zucchini and risoni and
simmer, stirring occasionally, for 5 minutes or until the risoni is almost
tender. Remove the pan from the heat and stir through the spinach
and peas. Stand, covered, for 3 minutes or until the risoni is tender.
Season to taste.

3 Divide the soup among four bowls, top with basil and serve.

DAIRY
FREE

GLUTEN
FREE

REFINED
SUGAR FREE

FREEZER
FRIENDLY

I could eat this RIGHT NOW . . .

JAPANESE DESK NOODLES

SERVES 4 — PREP 20 MINUTES / STAND 10 MINUTES — TOTAL CALORIES 497 / CALORIES PER SERVE 124

This recipe truly makes veggies the heroes. If you're serving these at home, simply
divide all of the ingredients among four large serving bowls, cover with plates or clean
tea towels and let them stand until the noodles are soft. Sweet potato glass noodles
are available in Asian grocers, though you can also use rice noodles.

1 garlic clove, crushed

**5 cm piece of ginger,
cut into matchsticks**

**3 tablespoons tamari
(gluten-free soy sauce)**

1 tablespoon white miso paste

**100 g sweet potato glass noodles,
roughly broken**

200 g firm tofu, cut into cubes

**300 g mixed Asian mushrooms,
trimmed and torn**

**½ bunch choy sum, trimmed,
stems finely sliced, leaves torn**

**1 long red chilli, finely sliced
on the diagonal**

1.5 litres boiling water

1 Place the garlic, ginger, tamari, miso and 3 tablespoons warm tap
water in a heatproof jug and stir until well combined. Divide the mixture
among four large heatproof, airtight portable lunch containers.

2 Add the noodles to the containers, then top with the tofu, mushrooms,
choy sum and chilli. Cover and chill overnight or for up to 3 days.

3 Transport the containers in portable chiller bags and keep chilled until
you are ready to serve. Remove the lid, pour 1½ cups boiling water into
each container and stir gently. Immediately return the lid and stand for
10 minutes or until the noodles have softened. Stir well and serve.

*WATCH OUT - your
colleagues will pinch
this for lunch.
Keep it well hidden!*

VEGAN
VEGETARIAN   DAIRY
FREE   GLUTEN
FREE   REFINED
SUGAR FREE   LUNCHBOX
FRIENDLY

This also makes a GREAT ENTREE for a DINNER PARTY.

CREAMY CELERY *and* FENNEL SOUP *with* PANEER CROUTONS

SERVES 4   PREP 20 MINUTES / COOK 20 MINUTES — TOTAL CALORIES 786 / CALORIES PER SERVE 197

If you've never tasted fennel I urge you to give it a go. The sweet, subtle aniseed
flavour is amazing. Paneer is a non-melting cheese popular in Indian cuisine.
You'll find it in larger supermarkets, alongside the haloumi and feta.

4 celery stalks, finely sliced

**4 baby fennel bulbs, trimmed
and finely sliced**

**1 litre Vegetable Stock
(see page 331)**

1 × 165 ml tin light coconut milk

100 g paneer, cut into cubes

½ teaspoon curry powder

coconut oil or olive oil cooking spray

⅓ cup small coriander leaves

1 Place the celery, fennel and stock in a large saucepan over high heat.
Bring to the boil, then reduce the heat to medium and simmer, covered
and stirring occasionally, for 15 minutes or until the vegetables are
just tender.

2 Add the coconut milk, then season to taste and stir until well combined.
Remove the pan from the heat and, using a hand-held blender, blend
until smooth. Keep warm.

3 Place the paneer and curry powder in a bowl and season to taste.
Spray lightly with cooking spray, then gently toss until well combined.

4 Heat a large non-stick frying pan over high heat. Add the paneer
and cook, stirring, for 2 minutes or until crispy and golden.

5 Divide the soup among four bowls. Top with the paneer croutons
and coriander leaves and serve warm.

VEGETARIAN   GLUTEN FREE   REFINED SUGAR FREE   LUNCHBOX FRIENDLY   FREEZER FRIENDLY

BUTTER BEAN *and* TOMATO SOUP

SERVES 4 — PREP 15 MINUTES / COOK 15 MINUTES — TOTAL CALORIES 1318 / CALORIES PER SERVE 330

One of my favourites for the cooler months.

**2 cups Tomato Passata
(see page 330)**

**1 litre Vegetable Stock
(see page 331)**

**2 × 400 g tins butter beans,
drained and rinsed**

**300 g green beans, trimmed
and cut into 3 cm lengths**

**½ quantity Nutty Herb Dressing
(see page 146)**

1 Place the passata, stock and butter beans in a large saucepan over high heat. Bring to the boil, then reduce the heat to medium and simmer, covered and stirring occasionally, for 10 minutes.

2 Add the green beans and continue to simmer, stirring occasionally, for 3 minutes or until the beans are just tender. Season to taste.

3 Divide the soup among four bowls. Spoon over the dressing and serve.

VEGAN
VEGETARIAN

DAIRY
FREE

GLUTEN
FREE

REFINED
SUGAR FREE

FREEZER
FRIENDLY

ROAST WINTER VEGETABLE *and* BACON SOUP

SERVES 4 — PREP 20 MINUTES / COOK 35 MINUTES — TOTAL CALORIES 724 / CALORIES PER SERVE 181

Put your woolly socks on!

2 parsnips, peeled and chopped

1 swede, peeled and chopped

1 turnip, peeled and chopped

2 carrot, chopped

400 g butternut pumpkin, peeled, seeded and chopped

1 tablespoon rosemary leaves, finely chopped

coconut oil or olive oil cooking spray

2 garlic cloves

2 rindless streaky bacon rashers, chopped

1 litre Chicken Stock (see page 331)

1 cup flat-leaf parsley leaves, chopped

1 Preheat the oven to 200°C (180°C fan forced). Line a large baking tray with baking paper.

2 Spread out the parsnip, swede, turnip, carrot, pumpkin and rosemary in a single layer on the prepared tray. Spray lightly with cooking spray and season to taste. Bake for 20 minutes, then add the garlic and bacon and bake for a further 10 minutes or until the vegetables are almost tender and the bacon is golden.

3 Transfer the vegetable mixture to a large saucepan. Add the stock and bring to the boil over high heat, then reduce the heat to medium and simmer, stirring occasionally, for 5 minutes or until the vegetables are very tender. Remove the pan from the heat.

4 Add the parsley, season to taste and stir until well combined. Divide among four bowls and serve warm.

PALEO	DAIRY FREE	GLUTEN FREE	REFINED SUGAR FREE	FREEZER FRIENDLY

Green Salads

Mix and match these suggestions for an abundant salad bowl:

	 +	
WATERCRESS LEAVES	CARROT	STRAWBERRIES
 +		
ROCKET LEAVES	BABY FENNEL	ORANGE
	 +	
MIXED SALAD LEAVES	BABY BEETROOT	CRAISINS
 +	 +	
KALE	CELERY	MIXED BABY TOMATOES
		 +
BABY SPINACH LEAVES	CAPSICUM	SEEDLESS RED GRAPES
 +	 +	
WOMBOK (CHINESE CABBAGE)	ZUCCHINI	PEAR

PROTEIN
↓

TOPPERS
↓

DRESSINGS
↓

(SEE PAGE 146 FOR DRESSINGS)

FIRM TOFU

FRESH HERBS

SWEET CHILLI DRESSING

COOKED CHICKEN BREAST

PINE NUTS

JAPANESE DRESSING

TINNED BLACK BEANS

ROLLED OATS

ITALIAN DRESSING

FRESH FULL-CREAM RICOTTA

MIXED CRUNCHY SPROUTS

NUTTY HERB DRESSING

COOKED QUINOA

MIXED SEEDS

CREAMY DRESSING

TINNED TUNA IN SPRINGWATER

TOASTED SPICES

LEMON VINAIGRETTE

LOVE a good potato salad . . .

PERI PERI POTATO SALAD

SERVES 4 — PREP 15 MINUTES / COOK 15 MINUTES — TOTAL CALORIES 922 / CALORIES PER SERVE 231

Peri peri is a spicy, citrusy chilli-based seasoning mix you'll find in the supermarket spice aisle. To cook your chicken, place two or three chicken tenderloins in a microwave-safe bowl and cover with cold tap water. Cover, then microwave on high for 3 minutes or until cooked, then drain.

500 g baby red potatoes, halved

3 teaspoons peri peri seasoning

extra virgin olive oil cooking spray

250 g grape tomatoes, halved lengthways

2 celery stalks, finely sliced

2 spring onions, finely sliced

100 g mixed salad leaves

200 g cooked chicken, chopped

1 quantity Lemon Vinaigrette (see page 146)

1 Place the potato in a saucepan and cover with cold tap water. Bring to the boil over high heat, then reduce the heat to medium and simmer for 12 minutes or until just cooked. Drain. Transfer to a large heatproof bowl or dish.

2 Add the peri peri seasoning to the potato and season to taste, then spray lightly with cooking spray and toss until well combined. Heat a large chargrill pan over high heat, add the potato and cook for 2 minutes, turning occasionally, until golden on the cut sides. Return to the heatproof bowl or dish.

3 Add the remaining ingredients to the hot potato mixture, season to taste and toss gently to combine. Divide among four plates and serve warm.

DAIRY FREE　　GLUTEN FREE　　REFINED SUGAR FREE　　LUNCHBOX FRIENDLY

ZUCCHINI TABBOULEH *and* CHARGRILLED VEGETABLES

SERVES 4 — PREP 20 MINUTES / STAND 20 MINUTES / COOK 10 MINUTES —
TOTAL CALORIES 582 / CALORIES PER SERVE 146

I just adore chargrilled veggies – I have them at least once a week, if not more.
Combining them with a super-tasty tabbouleh gives your body a cascade of nutrients.

1 zucchini, cut into 3 cm pieces

2 cups flat-leaf parsley leaves, chopped

1 cup mint leaves, chopped

1 bunch chives, chopped

2 tomatoes, finely chopped

1 quantity Lemon Vinaigrette (see page 146)

1 eggplant, cut into 3 cm pieces

1 yellow capsicum, seeded and cut into strips

1 small red onion, cut into rings

1 Place the zucchini in the bowl of a food processor and process until finely chopped into rice-sized pieces. Transfer to a large bowl.

2 Add the parsley, mint, chives, tomato and half the dressing to the zucchini and season to taste. Stir until well combined, then leave to stand at room temperature for 20 minutes.

3 Place the eggplant, capsicum and onion in a bowl. Add the remaining dressing, season to taste and toss until well combined.

4 Heat a large chargrill pan over high heat. Add the vegetable mixture in batches and chargrill for 3 minutes or until just tender and golden.

5 Divide the chargrilled vegetables among four plates, top with the tabbouleh and serve warm.

VEGAN VEGETARIAN   PALEO   DAIRY FREE   GLUTEN FREE   REFINED SUGAR FREE   LUNCHBOX FRIENDLY   FREEZER FRIENDLY

Because CHARGRILLS
are not just for
meat-eaters . . . .

YES, you can make
sushi at home!

SUSHI SALAD BOWLS

SERVES 4 — PREP 20 MINUTES / COOK 5 MINUTES + COOLING — TOTAL CALORIES 1203 / CALORIES PER SERVE 301

The great thing about these salad bowls (apart from the fact that they are super-tasty and nutritious) is that all of the ingredients are easy to find in major supermarkets. If you want to save time, packets of pre-sliced nori and roasted sesame seeds are available in Asian grocers.

1 × 250 g packet microwaveable brown basmati and wild rice

1 tablespoon seasoned rice wine vinegar (sushi vinegar)

1 carrot, cut into matchsticks

1 Lebanese cucumber, cut into matchsticks

1 small avocado, quartered

100 g finely sliced raw sashimi-grade salmon

1 sheet nori, cut into thin strips

1 tablespoon sesame seeds, roasted

1 quantity Japanese Dressing (see page 147)

2 tablespoons tamari (gluten-free soy sauce)

1 Heat the rice according to the packet instructions and transfer to a heatproof bowl. Stir in the vinegar, then leave to cool to room temperature, stirring occasionally.

2 Divide the rice among four bowls. Top with carrot, cucumber, avocado and salmon and sprinkle with the nori and sesame seeds. Drizzle the dressing over the top and serve with the tamari alongside.

GLUTEN FREE   REFINED SUGAR FREE   LUNCHBOX FRIENDLY

ISRAELI COUSCOUS SALAD

SERVES 4 — PREP 15 MINUTES / COOK 15 MINUTES + COOLING — TOTAL CALORIES 674 / CALORIES PER SERVE 169

Israeli couscous is also known as pearl couscous and has a pasta-like texture
when cooked. You can find it in the pasta aisle in major supermarkets. Feel free
to use chicken instead of the turkey, or even tofu if you want to go vegetarian.

⅓ cup Israeli couscous

**1 quantity Nutty Herb Dressing
(see page 146)**

1 cup small mint leaves

**4 radishes, very finely sliced
into rounds**

**1 Lebanese cucumber,
finely sliced into rounds**

**2 baby cos lettuce, trimmed,
finely sliced crossways**

50 g shaved turkey, torn

1 Place the couscous in a saucepan and cover with cold tap water.
Place the pan over high heat and bring to the boil, then reduce the
heat to medium and simmer, stirring occasionally, for 12 minutes
or until tender. Drain. Transfer to a heatproof bowl.

2 Add the dressing to the hot couscous and season to taste. Stir until well
combined, then leave to cool to room temperature, stirring occasionally.

3 Add the remaining ingredients to the couscous mixture and toss gently
to combine. Divide among four bowls and serve.

PALEO   DAIRY
FREE   REFINED
SUGAR FREE   LUNCHBOX
FRIENDLY

ALMOST NICOISE SALAD

SERVES 4 — PREP 25 MINUTES / COOK 25 MINUTES — TOTAL CALORIES 713 / CALORIES PER SERVE 178

Sweet potato is a great alternative to potato as it's high in nutrients,
especially vitamins A, C and E. It's delicious in this salad.

**200 g small sweet potato,
finely sliced into rounds**

extra virgin olive oil cooking spray

**1 radicchio, trimmed,
leaves separated and torn**

20 g mixed salad leaves

**100 g baby green beans, trimmed,
finely sliced on the diagonal**

**8 pitted kalamata olives,
halved lengthways**

**100 g sashimi-grade tuna,
very finely sliced**

**1 quantity Lemon Vinaigrette
(see page 146)**

1 Preheat the oven to 200°C (180°C fan-forced) and line a baking tray
with baking paper.

2 Place the sweet potato on the prepared tray, then spray lightly with
cooking spray and season to taste. Bake for 25 minutes or until tender
and golden. Allow to cool slightly on the tray.

3 Meanwhile, divide the radicchio, salad leaves, beans, olives and tuna
among four plates.

4 Add the warm potato to the salad plates and drizzle with the lemon
vinaigrette. Season to taste and serve.

DAIRY
FREE

GLUTEN
FREE

REFINED
SUGAR FREE

LUNCHBOX
FRIENDLY

ROAST FENNEL *and* CARROT SALAD
with GOAT'S CHEESE

SERVES 4 — PREP 20 MINUTES / COOK 15 MINUTES + COOLING —
TOTAL CALORIES 746 / CALORIES PER SERVE 187

Different-coloured heirloom carrots look lovely in this autumn salad.

**4 baby fennel bulbs, trimmed
and quartered lengthways**

**2 bunches baby carrots, trimmed
and scrubbed**

**1 quantity Sweet Chilli Dressing
(see page 147)**

**3 tablespoons pecans,
roughly chopped**

4 witlof, trimmed, leaves separated

1 cup flat-leaf parsley leaves

50 g soft goat's cheese

1 Preheat the oven to 220°C (200°C fan-forced).

2 Place the fennel, carrot and dressing in a large baking dish, season
to taste and toss until well combined.

3 Roast for 15 minutes or until the vegetables are just tender and golden.
Remove from the oven. Add the pecans and gently toss together, then
leave to cool to room temperature.

4 Add the witlof and parsley to the carrot mixture and toss to combine.
Divide the salad among four plates, top with goat's cheese and serve.

VEGETARIAN   REFINED
SUGAR FREE   LUNCHBOX
FRIENDLY

ITALIAN DRESSING

MAKES ½ CUP (SERVES 6)
PREP 5 MINUTES
TOTAL CALORIES 291
CALORIES PER SERVE 49

2 tablespoons extra virgin olive oil
3 tablespoons balsamic vinegar
1 small garlic clove, thinly sliced
½ teaspoon mixed dried herbs

1 Place the all ingredients in a jar and season to taste. Seal the jar, then shake vigorously until well combined.

2 Use straight away or store in a cool, dark place for up to 2 weeks.

LEMON VINAIGRETTE

MAKES ½ CUP (SERVES 6)
PREP 5 MINUTES
TOTAL CALORIES 264
CALORIES PER SERVE 44

2 teaspoons finely grated lemon zes
3 tablespoons fresh lemon juice
1 teaspoon dijon mustard
2 tablespoons olive oil
freshly ground white pepper

1 Place the lemon zest, juice and mustard in a bowl and whisk together until well combined.

2 While whisking vigorously, slowly pour in the oil until well incorporated and the dressing is thick and creamy. Season to taste with white pepper and salt.

3 Use straight away or store in an airtight container in the fridge for up to 1 week.

NUTTY HERB DRESSING

MAKES ⅔ CUP (SERVES 8)
PREP 5 MINUTES
TOTAL CALORIES 235
CALORIES PER SERVE 29

3 tablespoons red wine vinegar
1 tablespoon extra virgin olive oil
1 spring onion, finely chopped
2 tablespoons finely chopped flat-leaf parsley
2 tablespoons finely chopped basil
1 tablespoon shelled pistachios, finely chopped

1 Place all the ingredients and 1 tablespoon water in a bowl and stir until well combined. Season to taste.

2 Use straight away or store in an airtight container in the fridge for up to 1 week.

CREAMY DRESSING

MAKES ½ CUP (SERVES 6)
PREP 5 MINUTES
TOTAL CALORIES 126
CALORIES PER SERVE 21

1 garlic clove, chopped
½ teaspoon sea salt flakes
⅓ cup full-cream Greek yoghurt
1 tablespoon white wine vinegar
1 tablespoon finely chopped chives
freshly ground white pepper

1 Place the garlic on a board and
  sprinkle with the salt. Using a fork,
  mash together until the garlic turns
  to a paste. Transfer to a bowl.

2 Add the remaining ingredients and
  stir until well combined. Season to
  taste with white pepper.

3 Use straight away or store in an
  airtight container in the fridge for
  up to 1 week.

SWEET CHILLI DRESSING

MAKES ½ CUP (SERVES 6)
PREP 5 MINUTES + COOLING
TOTAL CALORIES 171
CALORIES PER SERVE 29

1 small red chilli, finely chopped
2 tablespoons honey
3 tablespoons boiling water
½ teaspoon sesame oil
1 tablespoon tamari
(gluten-free soy sauce)
1 tablespoon fresh lime juice

1 Place the chilli, honey and boiling
  water in a heatproof jug and stir until
  honey has dissolved. Set aside and
  allow to come to room temperature.

2 Stir in the remaining ingredients.

3 Use straight away or store in an airtight
  container in the fridge for up to 1 week.

JAPANESE DRESSING

MAKES ⅔ CUP (SERVES 8)
PREP 5 MINUTES
+ COOLING
TOTAL CALORIES 262
CALORIES PER SERVE 33

2 tablespoons Japanese
mayonnaise (kewpie)
½ teaspoon wasabi
3 teaspoons white miso paste

1 Place all the ingredients
  and ⅓ cup warm water in
  a heatproof jug and stir
  until well combined.

2 Use straight away or store in
  an airtight container in the
  fridge for up to 1 week.

YES, that's right –
BRUSSELS in
your OMELETTE!

FLUFFY OMELETTE *with* BRUSSELS SPROUTS

SERVES 1 — PREP 10 MINUTES / COOK 5 MINUTES — TOTAL CALORIES 269 / CALORIES PER SERVE 269

Don't be fooled by the simplicity of this little recipe – it is super-nutritious and will keep you going for hours. No need to cook your sprouts first – the residual heat from the omelette will warm them through.

2 eggs

1 egg white

1 teaspoon thyme leaves

2 tablespoons finely chopped flat-leaf parsley

1 tablespoon snipped chives

coconut oil or olive oil cooking spray

6 Brussels sprouts, very finely sliced

2 teaspoons pumpkin seeds

1   Place the eggs, egg white and 1 tablespoon water in a large bowl. Using a hand-held mixer, whisk on high speed for 2 minutes or until very foamy. Add the herbs and season to taste, then whisk until just combined.

2   Heat a 20 cm heavy-based frying pan over medium–high heat and spray lightly with cooking spray. Pour in the egg mixture. Using a heatproof spatula, slowly draw in the outer edges of slightly firm egg as it cooks to the centre of the pan for the first minute of cooking, then leave untouched for a further 1 minute or until the egg has set underneath and almost set on top.

3   Add the sprouts and pumpkin seeds to one half of the omelette, then carefully flip the other half over to cover the filling. Slide the omelette onto a plate and serve hot.

VEGETARIAN   PALEO   DAIRY FREE   GLUTEN FREE   REFINED SUGAR FREE

SUPERFOOD firing on all cylinders with this one.

CAULIFLOWER *and* BROCCOLI FRIED 'RICE'

SERVES 4 — PREP 20 MINUTES / COOK 10 MINUTES — TOTAL CALORIES 508 / CALORIES PER SERVE 127

Two of my favourite veggies in one delicious dish. This is a perfect recipe for people
trying to cut down on processed grains. I promise you – you won't even miss the rice!

400 g cauliflower, trimmed, stems chopped, florets removed

200 g broccoli, trimmed, stems chopped, florets removed

2 teaspoons sesame oil

2 garlic cloves, crushed

3 cm piece of ginger, finely grated

100 g raw prawn meat, chopped

2 eggs, whisked

½ cup frozen baby peas

2 tablespoons tamari (gluten-free soy sauce)

2 spring onions, finely sliced on the diagonal

1 Place the cauliflower and broccoli stems in the bowl of a food processor and process until finely chopped into rice-sized pieces. Transfer to a bowl. Repeat this process with the cauliflower and broccoli florets.

2 Heat the oil in a large wok over high heat, add the 'rice' and cook, tossing, for 2 minutes. Add the garlic, ginger and prawn meat and cook, tossing, for another 2 minutes.

3 Push the mixture to one side of the wok. Pour in the egg and cook, stirring, for 1 minute or until the egg has set. Add the peas and 1 tablespoon tamari and cook, tossing, for 2 minutes or until the 'rice' is cooked and light golden.

4 Divide the fried 'rice' among four plates and top with the spring onion. Serve warm with the remaining tamari alongside.

PALEO   DAIRY FREE   GLUTEN FREE   REFINED SUGAR FREE   LUNCHBOX FRIENDLY   FREEZER FRIENDLY

OMG I've died and gone to Vietnamese heaven. So CRISPY and DELICIOUS.

VIETNAMESE COCONUT PANCAKES
with SHREDDED PORK

SERVES 4 — PREP 20 MINUTES / CHILL 1 HOUR / COOK 15 MINUTES —
TOTAL CALORIES 786 / CALORIES PER SERVE 197

I'm cheating here, I know, but sometimes there isn't time to cook a roast on the weekend, plus slow-cooked shredded pork is readily available in large supermarkets.

½ cup rice flour

1 tablespoon gluten-free cornflour

1 teaspoon ground turmeric

1 × 165 ml tin light coconut milk

½ cup iced water

150 g slow-cooked shredded pork

1 cup bean sprouts, trimmed

1 cup mint leaves

1 cup Thai basil leaves

coconut oil or olive oil cooking spray

1 small lemon, cut into wedges

1 quantity Sweet Chilli Dressing
(see page 147)

1 Place the rice flour, cornflour, turmeric, coconut milk and iced water in a bowl. Season to taste, then whisk until smooth and well combined. Chill, covered, for 1 hour.

2 Combine the pork, sprouts and mint and basil leaves in a bowl.

3 Heat a small (16 cm) heavy-based non-stick frying pan over high heat and spray lightly with cooking spray. Pour one-quarter of the batter into the pan, tilting to cover the base and a little up the side, and cook, untouched, for 3 minutes or until golden and crisp on the underside.

4 Transfer the pancake to a plate and immediately top one half with a quarter of the pork mixture. Fold the untopped pancake half over to enclose and cover to keep warm. Repeat with the remaining batter and pork mixture to make four filled pancakes in total. Serve warm with lemon wedges and the sweet chilli dressing.

DAIRY FREE · GLUTEN FREE · REFINED SUGAR FREE

CHINESE CABBAGE WRAPS

SERVES 4 — PREP 20 MINUTES / STAND 5 MINUTES — TOTAL CALORIES 832 / CALORIES PER SERVE 208

So quick to make. I love the crunch of the cabbage and snow peas against the softness of the noodles. Brown rice vermicelli is more nutritious than white – look for it in larger supermarkets.

50 g brown rice vermicelli noodles, roughly broken into 5 cm lengths

boiling water, for soaking

100 g snow peas, cut into matchsticks

1 cup bean sprouts, trimmed

2 spring onions, finely sliced

1 tablespoon macadamias, roasted and finely chopped

300 g peeled cooked jumbo prawns, chopped

1 quantity Sweet Chilli Dressing (see page 147)

8 Chinese cabbage (wombok) leaves

1 Place the noodles in a large heatproof bowl. Cover with boiling water and stand for 5 minutes or until tender. Drain and rinse under cold running water, then drain again. Return to the same bowl.

2 Add the snow peas, sprouts, spring onion, macadamia, prawn and half the sweet chilli dressing to the noodles and toss to combine.

3 Lay the cabbage leaves flat on a clean work surface, the stem side closest to you. Divide the noodle mixture among the leaves, spooning it along the stem end. Roll up the leaves tightly to enclose the filling, leaving the sides open, then cut each roll in half. Arrange on four plates and serve with the remaining sweet chilli dressing on the side.

DAIRY FREE   GLUTEN FREE   REFINED SUGAR FREE   LUNCHBOX FRIENDLY

These are a CINCH after all that practise
bundling up Axel in muslin wraps!

CHICKEN CAESAR WRAP

SERVES 4 — PREP 20 MINUTES — TOTAL CALORIES 1053 / CALORIES PER SERVE 263

Mountain bread is very thin and dries out quickly, making it brittle and easy to break, so you need to have all of your filling ingredients ready to go and work with fast hands when rolling up. I use either poached or grilled chicken tenderloin meat.

4 pieces rice mountain bread

4 large butter lettuce leaves, trimmed and torn

4 soft-boiled eggs (see page 264), peeled and quartered lengthways

200 g cooked chicken, finely sliced

50 g shaved leg ham

2 celery stalks, finely sliced

2 tablespoons finely grated parmesan

½ quantity Creamy Dressing (see page 147)

1 Lay the mountain bread flat on a clean surface. Immediately top each one with a quarter of all the remaining ingredients, down the centre of the bread. Season to taste.

2 Roll up tightly to enclose the filling, leaving the ends open. Cut each roll in half and serve.

REFINED
SUGAR FREE

LUNCHBOX
FRIENDLY

CAJUN ROAST PUMPKIN *and* QUINOA SALAD

SERVES 4   PREP 20 MINUTES / COOK 35 MINUTES   TOTAL CALORIES 002 / CALORIES PER SERVE 204

Cajun seasoning is a spice blend containing paprika and cayenne pepper.
It's also great with barbecued meat.

**500 g kent pumpkin, seeded,
skin left on, cut into thin wedges**

3 teaspoons Cajun seasoning

extra virgin olive oil cooking spray

½ cup quinoa, rinsed well

**½ small iceberg lettuce,
cut into wedges**

100 g red cabbage, finely chopped

**1 quantity Creamy Dressing
(see page 147)**

**½ cup Fermented Slaw
(see page 332)**

1 Preheat the oven to 200°C (180°C fan-forced) and line a large baking tray with baking paper.

2 Place the pumpkin and seasoning in a bowl. Season to taste and lightly spray with cooking spray, then toss together until well combined. Spread out the pumpkin on the prepared tray in a single layer and roast, turning once, for 35 minutes or until cooked and golden.

3 Meanwhile, cook the quinoa in a saucepan of boiling water for 15 minutes or until tender. Drain well and transfer to a large heatproof bowl.

4 Add the hot pumpkin to the quinoa and toss gently to combine. Divide the pumpkin mixture and lettuce among four plates and top with the cabbage. Drizzle with the dressing and serve warm with fermented slaw alongside.

VEGETARIAN   GLUTEN FREE   REFINED SUGAR FREE   LUNCHBOX FRIENDLY

Lunchboxes

VEGGIE STICKS BABY CORN, BABY CARROTS, BROCCOLINI

AIR-POPPED POPCORN

SPICED TAMARI EDAMAME (PAGE 243)

PAPPADAMS

BOCCONCINI TOMS CHERRY TOMATOES, BOCCONCINI, BASIL LEAVES

MINI FLATBREADS (PAGE 118)

MIXED PITTED MARINATED OLIVES

THIN RICE CAKES

RAW GREENS WATERCRESS, SPROUTS, SHAVED BRUSSELS SPROUTS DRESSED WITH LIME JUICE

CURRY SEEDED CRACKERS (PAGE 260)

SESAME CUCUMBER NUGGETS (PAGE 257)

PLAIN RICE CRACKERS

PROTEIN ↓	FRUIT ↓	SWEET TREAT/ SNACK ↓
SMOKED SALMON WITH AVOCADO WEDGES	COTTAGE CHEESE + RED GRAPES	DATE LOAF (PAGE 287)
CHOPPED COOKED CHICKEN WITH CELERY + FROZEN BABY PEAS	FULL-CREAM GREEK YOGHURT WITH STRAWBERRIES	OVEN-DRIED FRUIT (PAGE 275)
CAULIFLOWER, HALOUMI AND PEA FRITTER (PAGE 117)	RED AND GREEN APPLE WEDGES TOSSED IN LEMON JUICE	LUNCHBOX OAT SLICE (PAGE 266)
HUMMUS WITH CHICKPEAS + POMEGRANATE SEEDS	WATERMELON, ROCKMELON + HONEYDEW MELON TOSSED WITH MINT	NO-BAKE GRANOLA (PAGE 91)
HONEY TAMARI MINI CHICKEN DRUMS	PEACH WEDGES + ORANGE SEGMENTS TOPPED WITH PINE NUTS	BLISS BALL (PAGE 304)
COOKED QUINOA TOSSED WITH BLACK BEANS	TRAFFIC LIGHT FRUIT SALAD: STRAWBERRIES, KIWI FRUIT, MANDARIN	DRIED FRUIT + NUT CHOC: CRAISINS, ALMONDS + 70% COCOA DARK CHOCOLATE

Risotto is notorious for being a high-cal dish... complete TURNAROUND with this HEALTHY one!

LEMONY KALE *and* BARLEY RISOTTO

SERVES 4 — PREP 15 MINUTES / COOK 45 MINUTES / STAND 3 MINUTES —
TOTAL CALORIES 896 / CALORIES PER SERVE 224

Barley has a whack of fibre and a decent amount of iron, magnesium and vitamin B6.
Combine that with leafy green kale and the antioxidant power of lemon and you've got
yourself one healthy meal. To make it vegetarian, simply use a vegetable stock.

20 g butter

1 garlic clove, crushed

**1 leek, halved lengthways,
finely sliced crossways**

½ cup pearl barley

1 litre Chicken Stock (see page 331)

**1 bunch kale, stalks removed,
leaves shredded**

**finely grated zest and juice
of 1 large lemon**

**2 tablespoons finely
grated parmesan**

1   Heat a large saucepan over medium heat, add the butter, garlic, leek and 3 tablespoons water and bring to a simmer. Simmer, stirring occasionally, for 5 minutes or until the leek is very soft.

2   Add the pearl barley and cook, stirring, for 2 minutes. Pour in half the stock and stir until the mixture reaches a simmer. Reduce the heat to low and simmer gently, partially covered and stirring occasionally, for 15 minutes or until all the stock has been absorbed.

3   Pour in the remaining stock and cook, stirring occasionally, for about 20 minutes or until all the stock has been absorbed and the barley is tender.

4   Remove the pan from the heat. Add the kale, lemon zest and juice and 1 tablespoon parmesan, season to taste and stir until well combined. Stand, covered, for 3 minutes or until the kale has wilted. Stir once more, then divide among four plates and sprinkle with the remaining parmesan. Serve warm.

REFINED
SUGAR FREE

FREEZER
FRIENDLY

She eats Rasta? HELL, YEAH!

MACERATED TOMATOES *with* BROKEN PASTA

SERVES 4 — PREP 10 MINUTES / STAND 20 MINUTES / COOK 5 MINUTES —
TOTAL CALORIES 678 / CALORIES PER SERVE 170

This little recipe is a deconstructed version of pasta with tomato sauce. I love how
it uses fresh ingredients prepared with a minimum of fuss. If you can't find angel
hair pasta, spaghetti will work too.

400 g mixed baby tomatoes, halved

1 tablespoon rosemary leaves, finely chopped

1 garlic clove, crushed

1 tablespoon avocado oil

1 cup basil leaves, torn

2 teaspoons baby capers, rinsed

100 g angel hair pasta, broken into quarters

100 g fresh full-cream ricotta, crumbled

1 Place the tomato, rosemary and garlic in a bowl and season to taste. Using clean hands, squeeze the tomato mixture together to release all the natural juices from the tomato.

2 Add the oil, basil and capers and stir until well combined. Stand at room temperature for 20 minutes.

3 Meanwhile, cook the pasta in a large saucepan of boiling water for 4 minutes or until just tender. Drain.

4 Add the hot pasta to the tomato mixture and toss to combine. Divide among four bowls, top with crumbled ricotta and serve warm.

VEGETARIAN   REFINED SUGAR FREE   LUNCHBOX FRIENDLY

A FUN FAMILY MEAL - the kids will love the help-yourself serving and the table will be BUZZING.

TOFU LARB *in* LETTUCE CUPS

SERVES 4 — PREP 15 MINUTES / COOK 5 MINUTES — TOTAL CALORIES 751 / CALORIES PER SERVE 188

Larb, the national dish of Laos, is minced meat seasoned with chilli, lemongrass,
fish sauce and lime. This vegetarian version is so incredibly flavoursome and easy
to prepare that it's sure to become a staple.

2 teaspoons coconut oil

100 g firm tofu, cut into cubes

1 bird's eye chilli, finely chopped

**2 lemongrass stalks, white part
only, finely chopped**

2 teaspoons fish sauce

finely grated zest and juice of 1 lime

½ cup mint leaves

½ cup coriander leaves

100 g brown rice vermicelli noodles

**2 baby gem lettuce, trimmed,
leaves separated**

**2 tablespoons salted peanuts,
finely chopped**

1 Melt the coconut oil in a wok over high heat, add the tofu, chilli and lemongrass and cook, tossing, for 3 minutes or until crisp and golden. Remove the wok from the heat.

2 Add the fish sauce, lime zest and juice, mint, coriander and noodles to the wok and toss gently to combine.

3 Divide the lettuce leaves among four plates. Spoon the tofu mixture into the leaves and sprinkle with the chopped peanuts. Serve warm.

VEGETARIAN   PALEO   DAIRY
FREE   GLUTEN
FREE   REFINED
SUGAR FREE   LUNCHBOX
FRIENDLY

GINGERED KALE *and* ASPARAGUS STIR-FRY *with* SICHUAN BEEF

SERVES 4 — PREP 20 MINUTES / COOK 5 MINUTES — TOTAL CALORIES 479 / CALORIES PER SERVE 120

I've always loved stir-fries, and this one features one of my all-time favourite veggies – asparagus. We used curly kale for this recipe because it looked so good, but feel free to use whichever variety you have to hand. Sichuan or Szechuan pepper is used in Chinese cooking. You'll find it in larger supermarkets and online.

2 teaspoons coconut oil

200 g beef fillet steak, halved horizontally and very finely sliced

2 teaspoons Sichuan pepper

4 spring onions, cut into 4 cm lengths

4 cm piece of ginger, cut into matchsticks

2 garlic cloves, finely sliced

300 g asparagus, trimmed, cut on the diagonal into 4 cm lengths

2 tablespoons tamari (gluten-free soy sauce)

2 large kale leaves, stalks removed, leaves shredded

1 Heat a wok over high heat and add the coconut oil. Once melted, add the beef, Sichuan pepper, spring onion, ginger and garlic and cook, tossing, for 2 minutes or until the beef is just cooked.

2 Add the asparagus and tamari and cook, tossing, for 1 minute or until the asparagus is just tender.

3 Remove the wok from the heat, add the kale and toss until well combined and the kale has wilted. Divide among four bowls and serve warm.

PALEO   DAIRY FREE   GLUTEN FREE   REFINED SUGAR FREE   LUNCHBOX FRIENDLY   FREEZER FRIENDLY

BEEF *and* BEETROOT *on* RYE

SERVES 4 — PREP 20 MINUTES — TOTAL CALORIES 1357 / CALORIES PER SERVE 339

So simple, so delicious.

1 large beetroot, peeled and coarsely grated

½ quantity Japanese Dressing (see page 147)

8 × 1 cm thick slices rye sourdough, toasted

150 g finely sliced rare roast beef

2 Lebanese cucumbers, peeled into ribbons

2 cups watercress leaves

4 golden shallots, finely sliced

1 lime, cut into wedges

1 Place the beetroot and dressing in a bowl and mix together well.

2 Put half the bread on serving plates. Top with the beetroot mixture, beef, cucumber and watercress. Sprinkle with shallot and sandwich with the remaining bread slices. Serve with lime wedges alongside.

REFINED SUGAR FREE   LUNCHBOX FRIENDLY

CITRUS COUSCOUS *with* BRUSSELS SPROUTS

SERVES 4   PREP 20 MINUTES / STAND 4 MINUTES — TOTAL CALORIES 867 / CALORIES PER SERVE 217

Brussels sprouts are so surprisingly sweet when raw, especially when served with all this great immunity-building citrus. I promise you'll fall in love!

½ cup instant wholemeal couscous

3 tablespoons craisins

2 cups boiling water

1 quantity Nutty Herb Dressing (see page 146)

1 orange, finely zested, then peeled and cut into segments

200 g Brussels sprouts, very finely shredded

2 cups watercress sprigs

50 g shaved turkey, finely sliced

1 Place the couscous, craisins and boiling water in a heatproof bowl. Stir with a fork, then immediately cover with a clean tea towel and stand for 3 minutes. Fluff with a fork again and stand, covered, for 1 minute. Fluff the grains one more time.

2 Add the dressing and orange zest, season to taste and stir until well combined.

3 Finally, add the orange segments, sprouts, watercress and turkey. Toss gently, then divide among four bowls and serve.

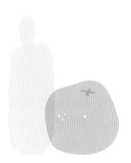

DAIRY
FREE

LUNCHBOX
FRIENDLY

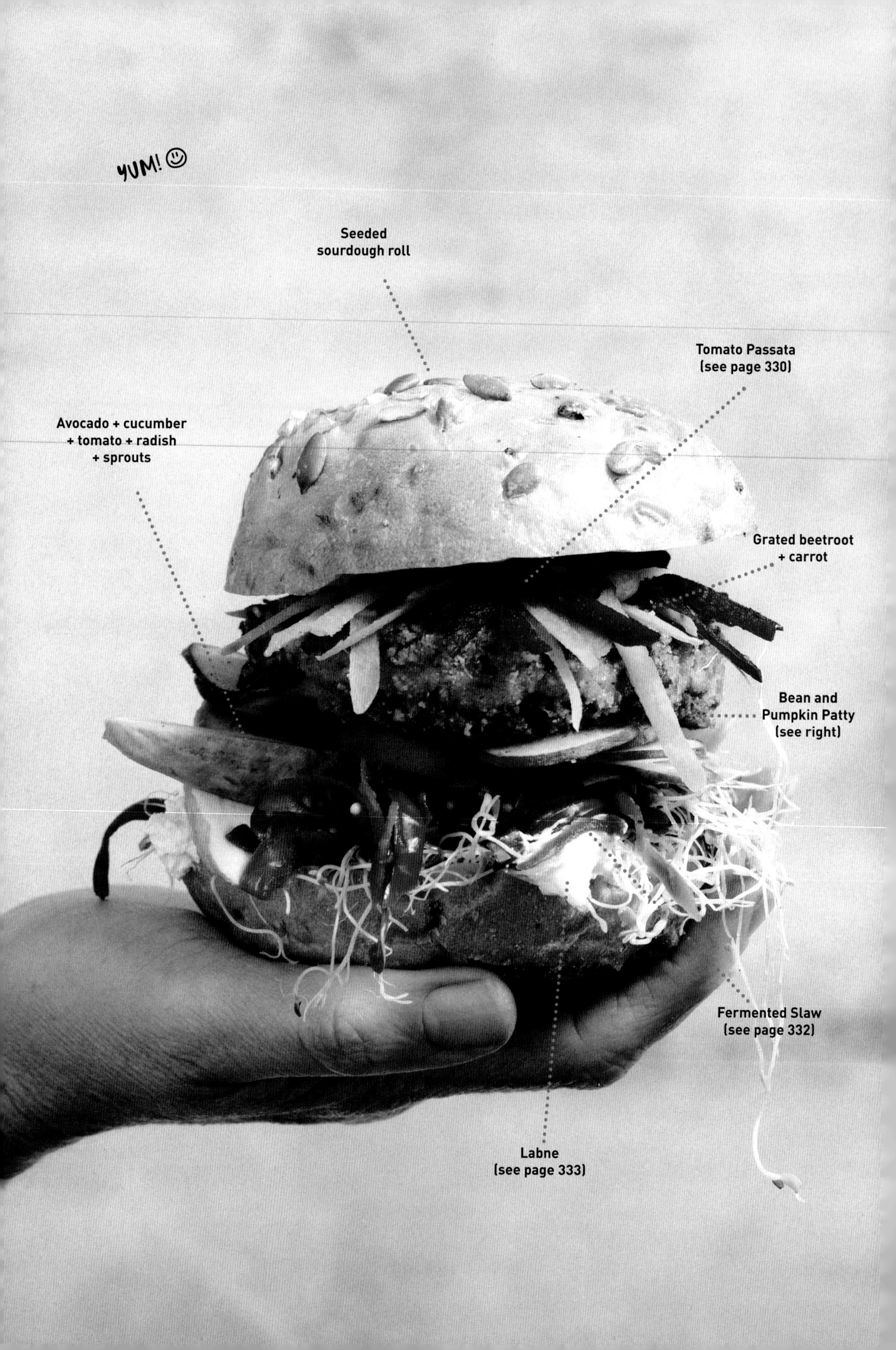

YUM! ☺

Seeded
sourdough roll

Tomato Passata
(see page 330)

Avocado + cucumber
+ tomato + radish
+ sprouts

Grated beetroot
+ carrot

Bean and
Pumpkin Patty
(see right)

Fermented Slaw
(see page 332)

Labne
(see page 333)

Burger
BUILDER

Try these combos:

+ BUNS

- ▶ Small seeded sourdough rolls
- ▶ Lightly chargrilled large field mushrooms
- ▶ Sliced gluten-free bread
- ▶ Traditional burger buns

+ PATTIES

- ▶ **Kanga Burger:** Spice kangaroo mince with garlic and chilli, shape into patties and chargrill over medium heat for 10 minutes.

- ▶ **Crispy Fish:** Coat boneless small white fish fillets in seasoned rice flour and pan-fry over medium heat for 4 minutes each side until crispy.

- ▶ **Bean and Pumpkin:** Mash together 1 x 400 g tin red kidney beans, drained and rinsed, with ½ cup cooled steamed pumpkin, 1 egg yolk, 1 tablespoon chia seeds and 1 tablespoon coconut flour. Shape into patties and cook under a hot grill for 2 minutes each side or until golden and heated through.

- ▶ **Chive Omelette:** Whisk 1 egg with 2 teaspoons water and 1 tablespoon finely chopped chives. Cook in a dry non-stick frying pan over medium heat for 2 minutes, then slide out, season and fold into quarters.

- ▶ **Sticky Tofu Steak:** Coat thickly sliced firm tofu with tamari (gluten-free soy sauce) and pure maple syrup, then pan-fry for 2 minutes each side until heated through, golden and sticky.

+ FILLINGS

- ▶ Avocado slices
- ▶ Greens – baby spinach, watercress, mixed salad leaves, rocket, baby kale
- ▶ Low-cal veggies – sliced tomato, cucumber, zucchini ribbons, sprouts, finely sliced celery, grated beetroot, grated carrot, sliced radish
- ▶ Cheese – finely grated parmesan, ricotta, Labne (see page 333)
- ▶ Fermented Slaw (see page 332)

+ SAUCES

- ▶ Tomato Passata (see page 330)
- ▶ Sweet Chilli Dressing (see page 147)
- ▶ Japanese Dressing (see page 147)
- ▶ Nutty Herb Dressing (see page 146)

PICKLED ONION *and* SILVERBEET
with SARDINES

SERVES 4 — PREP 15 MINUTES / STAND 1 HOUR / COOK 10 MINUTES —
TOTAL CALORIES 639 / CALORIES PER SERVE 160

Fresh sardines are packed with omega-3 fatty acids, vitamins and
minerals. Ask your fishmonger to clean them for you.

**finely grated zest and juice
of 1 large lemon**

1 small red onion, finely chopped

**1 bunch silverbeet, stalks removed,
leaves shredded**

**2 tablespoons French tarragon
leaves**

2 tablespoons pine nuts, roasted

extra virgin olive oil cooking spray

8 fresh whole sardines, cleaned

1 Place the lemon zest and juice and onion in a bowl and season to taste.
   Stand, covered, at room temperature for 1 hour or until the onion
   is very soft.

2 Heat a large deep frying pan over high heat. Add the silverbeet and
   2 tablespoons water and cook, tossing, for 2 minutes or until the leaves
   are just beginning to wilt. Remove from the heat. Season to taste, then
   stir through the tarragon and pine nuts. Cover to keep warm.

3 Preheat a grill to high. Line a baking tray with foil and lightly spray the
   foil with cooking spray. Place the sardines on the prepared tray, skin-
   side up, lightly spray with cooking spray and season to taste. Cook
   under the grill, carefully turning once, for 5 minutes or until just cooked
   and light golden.

4 Divide the silverbeet mixture among four plates, top with the sardines
   and drizzle with the pickled onion. Serve warm.

*I love sardines -
they pack a HUGE
NUTRITIONAL punch
and contain great
HEALTHY FATS.*

PALEO DAIRY FREE GLUTEN FREE REFINED SUGAR FREE

PUMPKIN *with* CHIMICHURRI LENTILS

SERVES 4 — PREP 20 MINUTES / STAND 30 MINUTES / COOK 20 MINUTES —
TOTAL CALORIES 967 / CALORIES PER SERVE 242

Chimichurri is an Argentinean spicy green sauce traditionally served with
barbecued meats. This vegan version has the same delicious ingredients –
they're just not blitzed to a paste.

**200 g peeled butternut pumpkin,
cut lengthways into 5 mm slices**

1 teaspoon cayenne pepper

2 teaspoons cumin seeds

coconut oil or olive oil cooking spray

3 tablespoons sliced almonds

CHIMICHURRI LENTILS

1 cup flat-leaf parsley leaves

½ cup coriander leaves

1 small garlic clove, crushed

¼ teaspoon dried chilli flakes

½ teaspoon dried oregano leaves

2 tablespoons red wine vinegar

2 teaspoons extra virgin olive oil

**1 × 400 g tin brown lentils,
drained and rinsed**

1 To make the chimichurri lentils, put all the ingredients in a bowl,
season to taste and mix well. Stand at room temperature, stirring
occasionally, for 30 minutes.

2 Meanwhile, preheat the oven to 220°C (200°C fan-forced) and line
a large baking tray with baking paper.

3 Place the pumpkin, cayenne and cumin in a bowl. Season to taste and
spray lightly with cooking spray, then toss until well combined. Spread
the pumpkin mixture over the prepared tray in a single layer and bake
for 20 minutes or until the pumpkin is tender and golden.

4 Divide the pumpkin among four plates and top with the chimichurri
lentils and a sprinkling of almonds. Serve warm.

VEGAN VEGETARIAN   DAIRY FREE   GLUTEN FREE   REFINED SUGAR FREE   LUNCHBOX FRIENDLY

VEGETARIAN ✓
HEARTY ✓
GREAT ZINGY TASTE ✓

SPROUTS *and* PEAS *with* LEMON PEPPER SQUID

SERVES 4 — PREP 15 MINUTES / COOK 5 MINUTES — TOTAL CALORIES 687 / CALORIES PER SERVE 172

This has got to be one of the easiest meals around. Plus it has peas, fresh
seafood and three kinds of sprouts – your body will thank you.

**finely grated zest and juice
of 1 large lemon**

**1 teaspoon freshly ground
white pepper**

500 g cleaned baby squid, scored

200 g mixed crunchy sprouts

½ cup alfalfa sprouts

**200 g Brussels sprouts,
finely sliced into rounds**

**½ cup frozen baby peas,
at room temperature**

1 tablespoon avocado oil

1 Place the lemon zest, pepper and squid in a bowl, season to taste with
salt and toss until well combined.

2 Combine the sprouts, Brussels sprouts, peas, oil and lemon juice in
a bowl and season to taste. Set aside.

3 Heat a large chargrill pan over high heat. Add the squid and cook for
2 minutes, turning occasionally, until just tender and light golden.

4 Divide the sprout salad among four plates, top with the squid and
serve warm.

PALEO   DAIRY
FREE   GLUTEN
FREE   REFINED
SUGAR FREE

Dinner

It's a HUG in a BOWL -
so warming for the SOUL.

POACHED SPRING VEGETABLES *with* CRISPY SKIN CHICKEN

SERVES 4 — PREP 20 MINUTES / COOK 20 MINUTES / STAND 5 MINUTES —
TOTAL CALORIES 950 / CALORIES PER SERVE 238

Those of you familiar with my other books might think I've lost my marbles with this recipe – not only is the skin left on, but it's crispy! Relax: there are no oils used for cooking, and the veggies are poached in a separate pan. Enjoy!

400 g chicken thigh fillets with skin on, skin scored and seasoned

1 litre Chicken Stock (see page 331)

2 tablespoons French tarragon leaves

2 teaspoons thyme leaves

4 fresh bay leaves

2 garlic cloves, finely sliced

2 bunches heirloom baby carrots, trimmed, skins scrubbed

100 g baby beans, trimmed

150 g asparagus, trimmed, halved lengthways

½ cup fresh peas

1 Preheat the oven to 200°C (180°C fan-forced).

2 Heat a large heavy-based ovenproof frying pan over medium heat. Add the chicken, skin-side down, and cook, untouched, for 10 minutes or until the skin is golden and crispy. Turn the chicken over, then transfer the pan to the oven and bake for 10 minutes or until the chicken is cooked. Remove from the oven and rest in the pan for 5 minutes. Transfer to a heatproof board and thickly slice.

3 Meanwhile, place the stock, herbs and garlic in a deep frying pan over high heat. Bring to the boil, then reduce the heat to medium and simmer for 5 minutes. Add the carrots and simmer for 3 minutes, then add the beans and asparagus and simmer for 1 minute. Remove the pan from the heat, stir in the peas and season to taste. Stand, covered, for 2 minutes.

4 Divide the vegetable mixture among shallow bowls and top with the chicken. Serve warm.

DAIRY FREE   GLUTEN FREE   REFINED SUGAR FREE   FREEZER FRIENDLY

ZUCCHINI *and* FENNEL CHICKEN LOAF

SERVES 4 — PREP 20 MINUTES / STAND 10 MINUTES / COOK 50 MINUTES —
TOTAL CALORIES 956 / CALORIES PER SERVE 239

I love this loaf. Make two and freeze one (slice it first and separate the slices
with baking paper). You can buy micro herbs from the fresh herb section in
major supermarkets, but any fresh herb will do.

2 zucchini, coarsely grated

1 carrot, coarsely grated

200 g chicken mince

2 eggs, whisked

2 tablespoons coconut flour

½ cup cooked brown basmati rice

3 teaspoons fennel seeds

**2 tablespoons pistachio kernels,
finely chopped**

**mixed green salad leaves and
micro herbs (optional), to serve**

1 Preheat the oven to 200°C (180°C fan-forced). Line the base and sides
of a 20 cm × 10 cm loaf tin with baking paper.

2 Place the zucchini, carrot, mince, egg, flour, rice and 2 teaspoons
fennel seeds in a large bowl. Season to taste and mix with your hands
until well combined. Press the mixture firmly into the prepared tin and
level the surface. Sprinkle the pistachios and remaining fennel seeds
over the top.

3 Bake for 50 minutes or until cooked and golden. To test, insert a skewer
in the centre – the cooking juices should run clear. Remove from the
oven, cover loosely with foil and rest for 10 minutes. Transfer the loaf
to a heatproof board and cut into slices. Serve warm with salad leaves,
sprinkled with micro herbs.

DAIRY FREE · GLUTEN FREE · REFINED SUGAR FREE · LUNCHBOX FRIENDLY · FREEZER FRIENDLY

A much HEALTHIER alternative to TAKEOUT . . .

THAI EGGPLANT SALAD *with* FISHCAKES

SERVES 4 — PREP 25 MINUTES / CHILL 30 MINUTES / COOK 10 MINUTES —
TOTAL CALORIES 615 / CALORIES PER SERVE 154

These gorgeous little fishcakes are so addictive – you'll want to double
the mixture so you've got enough for lunch the next day.

150 g white fish fillets (dory or snapper), skin and bones removed, roughly chopped

2 kaffir lime leaves, centre vein removed, finely chopped

2 tablespoons iced water

1 quantity Sweet Chilli Dressing (see page 147)

4 baby eggplants, trimmed, halved lengthways

100 g snake beans, trimmed, halved crossways

coconut oil or olive oil cooking spray

1 telegraph cucumber, halved lengthways, seeds scraped, finely sliced on the diagonal

1 carrot, cut into matchsticks

½ cup coriander leaves

½ cup mint leaves

1 Line a baking tray with baking paper. Place the fish, kaffir lime leaf, iced water and 1 tablespoon of the dressing in the bowl of a food processor. Process until the mixture is smooth and well combined and feels sticky. With clean damp hands, roll 1 tablespoon measures of the fish mixture into flat 4 cm rounds. Place on the prepared tray and chill for 30 minutes to set firm.

2 Pour the remaining dressing into a large heatproof bowl and set aside.

3 Preheat a large chargrill pan over high heat. Add the eggplant and beans and cook, turning occasionally, for 3 minutes or until just tender and golden. Transfer to the bowl and toss through the dressing.

4 Lightly spray the fishcakes with cooking spray, then chargrill on the same pan for 2 minutes each side or until cooked and golden. Add to the bowl with the vegetables and toss well to combine.

5 Add the cucumber, carrot, coriander and mint to the bowl and toss again to combine. Divide the salad among four plates and serve warm.

DAIRY FREE   GLUTEN FREE   REFINED SUGAR FREE   LUNCHBOX FRIENDLY   FREEZER FRIENDLY

ITALIAN ROAST CAPSICUM *with* SNAPPER *and* WILD RICE CRUMB

SERVES 4 — PREP 20 MINUTES / COOK 25 MINUTES / STAND 5 MINUTES —
TOTAL CALORIES 1287 / CALORIES PER SERVE 322

Wild rice is not actually rice, but a member of the grass family. It has a lovely, nutty texture. To cook it, rinse it briefly, then bring to the boil with three times as much water and simmer for 45 minutes to 1 hour.

1 red capsicum, seeded and sliced into rings

1 green capsicum, seeded and sliced into rings

1 yellow capsicum, seeded and sliced into rings

1 quantity Italian Dressing (see page 146)

1 cup cooked wild rice

50 g Danish feta, crumbled

50 g pitted Sicilian green olives, roughly chopped

4 × 100 g dory fillets, skin and bones removed

1 Preheat the oven to 220°C (200°C fan-forced)

2 Place the capsicum rings and half the dressing in a baking dish and toss until well combined. Roast for 10 minutes.

3 Meanwhile, mix together the rice, feta, olives and remaining dressing in a bowl. Season to taste and mix again.

4 Place the fish on top of the capsicum in the dish and season to taste. Spoon the rice mixture evenly over the fillets and roast for 15 minutes or until the fish flakes easily when tested with a fork. Rest in the dish for 5 minutes, then serve warm.

GLUTEN FREE REFINED SUGAR FREE FREEZER FRIENDLY

NASI GORENG VEGETABLES *with* FRIED QUAIL EGGS

SERVES 4 - PREP 25 MINUTES / COOK 5 MINUTES — TOTAL CALORIES 566 / CALORIES PER SERVE 142

Save time by using your food processor to finely chop your vegetables. Simply cut them into rough 3 cm pieces and process separately, and in batches, until finely chopped. You'll find sambal oelek and kecap manis in Asian supermarkets.

2 Lebanese cucumbers, peeled into ribbons

250 g cherry tomatoes, sliced into rounds

½ cup small coriander sprigs

1 tablespoon coconut oil

12 quail eggs

1 carrot, finely chopped

2 celery stalks, finely chopped

4 yellow squash, finely chopped

1 bunch choy sum, trimmed and finely chopped

2 teaspoons sambal oelek (chilli paste)

2 tablespoons kecap manis (Indonesian sweet soy sauce)

1 Place the cucumber, tomato and coriander in a bowl. Toss gently together and chill until required.

2 Heat half the oil in a large heavy-based non-stick frying pan over medium heat. Once melted, carefully crack the quail eggs into the pan and cook, untouched, for 3 minutes or until the whites have set and crisped up and the yolks are still runny.

3 Meanwhile, heat the remaining oil in a large wok over high heat. Once melted, add the remaining ingredients and 2 tablespoons water and cook, tossing, for 2 minutes or until the vegetables are just tender, lightly crisp and light golden. Season to taste with pepper

4 Divide the vegetable mixture among four shallow bowls and top with the quail eggs. Arrange the cucumber salad alongside and serve warm.

VEGETARIAN

DAIRY FREE

GARLIC MUSHROOMS, CELERIAC SMASH *and* PEPPERED STEAK

SERVES 4 — PREP 20 MINUTES / STAND 5 MINUTES / COOK 25 MINUTES —
TOTAL CALORIES 997 / CALORIES PER SERVE 249

A protein-rich, low-GI take on the old steak and mash.
The garlic mushrooms are to die for!

300 g celeriac, peeled and chopped

2 carrots, sliced

400 g trimmed beef sirloin

1 tablespoon cracked black pepper

250 g portobello mushrooms, sliced

150 g mixed exotic mushrooms, separated, torn in half

200 g swiss brown mushrooms, halved

2 garlic cloves, finely sliced

½ cup Chicken Stock (see page 331)

20 g butter

2 spring onions, finely sliced

1 tablespoon thyme leaves

1 Place the celeriac and carrot in a saucepan and cover with cold tap water. Bring to the boil over high heat, then reduce the heat to medium–high and simmer rapidly for 15 minutes or until the vegetables are tender. Drain. Return to the pan, off the heat, and mash roughly together. Season to taste. Cover to keep warm.

2 Heat a chargrill pan over medium–high heat. Coat the steak on both sides with pepper and season to taste with salt. Chargrill for 2 minutes each side for medium–rare or until cooked to your liking. Transfer to a heatproof board, cover with foil and rest for 5 minutes, then finely slice.

3 Meanwhile, heat a large heavy-based non-stick frying pan over high heat. Add the mushrooms and cook, tossing, for 2 minutes. Add the garlic and stock and cook, stirring, for 1 minute. Remove the pan from the heat. Stir through the butter until melted, then stir in the spring onion and thyme and season to taste.

4 Divide the celeriac smash among four plates. Top with the steak and any resting juices, and spoon over the garlic mushrooms. Serve warm.

This is PUB GRUB at its best - PERFECT MANFOOD!

PALEO

GLUTEN FREE

REFINED SUGAR FREE

EGGPLANT PIZZA BASE

Halve 2 eggplants lengthways and chargrill over medium heat for 10 minutes, turning occasionally, until golden and just cooked. Spread the cut sides evenly with 1 cup Tomato Passata (see page 330). Top with your choice of toppings. Season to taste.

TOTAL CALORIES 230
CALORIES PER SERVE 58

Topping One:
1 x 400 g tin chickpeas, drained and rinsed
½ cup drained red pepper strips
½ cup pitted kalamata olives
50 g crumbled Danish feta
½ cup small flat-leaf parsley leaves

TOTAL CALORIES 722
CALORIES PER SERVE 181

ZUCCHINI PIZZA BASE

Combine 4 coarsely grated zucchini, 2 tablespoons grated parmesan, 1 egg and 2 tablespoons wholemeal self-raising flour and season to taste. Heat a small non-stick frying pan over medium heat. Spray lightly with oil. Press a quarter of the mixture into the pan, shaping it into an oval about 12 cm. Cook for 4 minutes, then flip over and cook for 4 minutes. Transfer to a plate and cover to keep warm. Repeat with the remaining mixture to make four bases. Sprinkle over an extra tablespoon of parmesan, then top with your choice of toppings. Season to taste.

TOTAL CALORIES 296
CALORIES PER SERVE 74

Topping One:
2 cups baby spinach leaves
8 torn baby bocconcini
½ cup basil leaves
lemon wedges, to serve

TOTAL CALORIES 180
CALORIES PER SERVE 45

BAGUETTE PIZZA BASE

Cut four 85 g mini baguettes in half horizontally and toast them. Spread the cut surfaces evenly with ½ cup Tomato Passata (see page 330). Top with your choice of toppings. Season to taste.

TOTAL CALORIES 895
CALORIES PER SERVE 224

Topping One:
4 grilled streaky bacon rashers
1 small pear, sliced
100 g shaved Brussels sprouts
30 g crumbled blue cheese

TOTAL CALORIES 489
CALORIES PER SERVE 122

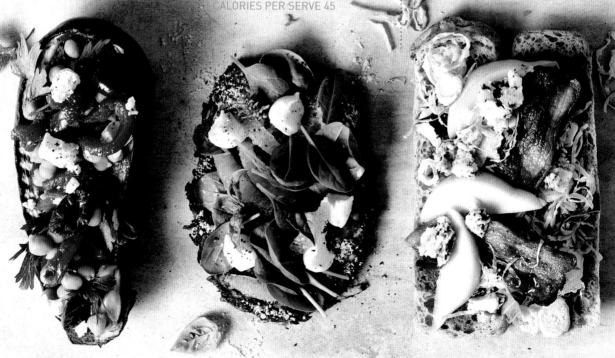

EGGPLANT PIZZA

Topping Two:

1 x 425 g tin tuna in
springwater, flaked
50 g chopped sun-dried
tomato
½ cup pitted Sicilian green
olives
50 g crumbled Danish feta
2 tablespoons chopped flat-
leaf parsley

TOTAL CALORIES 858
CALORIES PER SERVE 215

ZUCCHINI PIZZA

Topping Two:

4 tomatoes, sliced
4 thin slices prosciutto
1 large bocconcini, sliced
½ cup basil leaves
lemon wedges, to serve

TOTAL CALORIES 360
CALORIES PER SERVE 90

BAGUETTE PIZZA

Topping Two:

1 bunch asparagus,
pan-fried
4 halved figs
30 g crumbled blue cheese
1 cup watercress

TOTAL CALORIES 240
CALORIES PER SERVE 60

PASTA PIZZA BASE

Cook 125 g dried fettuccine in boiling water for 8 minutes or until just tender. Drain and transfer to a heatproof bowl. Add 2 whisked eggs and ½ cup grated tasty cheese. Season to taste and toss together until well combined. Line two large baking trays with baking paper. Form the mixture into four even mounds on the prepared trays, shaping them into ovals about 12 cm. Bake in a 220°C (200°C fan-forced) oven for 15 minutes, swapping the trays halfway through cooking, until cooked and golden. Spread the bases evenly with ½ cup ready-made red capsicum dip. Top with your choice of toppings. Season to taste.

TOTAL CALORIES 800
CALORIES PER SERVE 200

Topping One:

1 cup steamed chopped pumpkin
1 small red onion, finely sliced
50 g goat's cheese
1 tablespoon chopped chives

TOTAL CALORIES 279
CALORIES PER SERVE 70

MINI FLATBREAD PIZZA BASE

Spread 12 x 14 g mini wholemeal pita breads with ½ cup ready-made pizza sauce. Top with your choice of toppings. Transfer to two large baking trays lined with baking paper and bake in a 220°C (200°C fan-forced) oven for 5 minutes or until the cheese is melted and golden.

TOTAL CALORIES 523
CALORIES PER SERVE 131

Topping One:

½ green capsicum, finely chopped
125 g halved cherry tomatoes
½ cup grated tasty cheese

TOTAL CALORIES 239
CALORIES PER SERVE 60

BROCCO-FLOWER PIZZA BASE

Process 350 g cauliflower and 350 g broccoli in a food processor until finely chopped like rice. Transfer to a large bowl. Add 6 whisked eggs and ½ cup almond meal, and season to taste. Line two large baking trays with baking paper. Form the mixture into four even mounds on the prepared trays, shaping them into ovals about 12 cm in length. Bake in a 220°C (200°C fan-forced) oven for 20 minutes, swapping the trays halfway through cooking, until cooked and golden. Spread the bases evenly with ½ cup ready-made pesto (or homemade if you have some). Top with your choice of toppings. Season to taste.

TOTAL CALORIES 940
CALORIES PER SERVE 235

Topping One:

12 chargrilled peeled prawns
1 long green chilli, sliced
50 g crumbled fresh full-cream ricotta
1 tablespoon dill fronds
lemon wedges, to serve

TOTAL CALORIES 168
CALORIES PER SERVE 42

PASTA PIZZA

Topping Two:
50 g finely chopped cooked cured chorizo
1 small red onion, finely sliced
50 g goat's cheese
1 tablespoon chopped chives

TOTAL CALORIES 320
CALORIES PER SERVE 80

MINI FLATBREAD PIZZA

Topping Two:
50 g chopped shaved ham
100 g chopped pineapple
½ cup grated tasty cheese

TOTAL CALORIES 269
CALORIES PER SERVE 67

BROCCO-FLOWER PIZZA

Topping Two:
4 chargrilled portobello mushrooms, sliced
1 tablespoon thyme leaves
50 g crumbled fresh full-cream ricotta
50 g baby rocket
lemon wedges, to serve

TOTAL CALORIES 170
CALORIES PER SERVE 43

CHILLI GREEN BEANS *with* PORK

SERVES 4 — PREP 10 MINUTES / COOK 15 MINUTES — TOTAL CALORIES 455 / CALORIES PER SERVE 114

This is my kind of fast food: leafy greens, legumes, a dignified amount of meat protein
and plenty of kick. Oh, and I did mention that it's simple and quick? The chilli sauce and
Chinese cooking wine are available from larger supermarkets and Asian grocers.

150 g pork mince

500 g baby green beans, trimmed

**1 bunch baby bok choy, trimmed,
finely sliced lengthways**

2 garlic cloves, finely sliced

1 tablespoon Sriracha (chilli sauce)

**1 tablespoon Chinese cooking
wine (shaoxing)**

**2½ tablespoons tamari
(gluten-free soy sauce)**

1 Heat a large wok over high heat, add the pork and beans and cook,
   tossing, for 10 minutes or until cooked through, crisp and very golden.

2 Add the bok choy, garlic, chilli sauce, cooking wine and 2 teaspoons
   tamari and toss for 2 minutes or until the bok choy has wilted and
   the sauce has thickened.

3 Divide among four bowls and serve warm with the remaining tamari.

DAIRY
FREE

GLUTEN
FREE

REFINED
SUGAR FREE

The BETTER (and faster) way
to ENJOY TAKEOUT at home.

This is THE DISH that you PULL out of the oven and everyone goes 'OOOHHH' and 'AAAHHH'!

SUPER GREENS *and* SALMON BAKE *with* CAULIFLOWER CRUMB

SERVES 4 — PREP 20 MINUTES / STAND 10 MINUTES / COOK 35 MINUTES —
TOTAL CALORIES 1157 / CALORIES PER SERVE 289

This is a thoroughly delicious take on my favourite fish, plus I love being able to plonk
a casserole in the oven. If you can't find rainbow chard (it's like silverbeet only with red,
yellow, pink and purple stalks), just use silverbeet.

2 × 165 ml tins light coconut milk

1 garlic clove, crushed

**1 large bunch kale, stalks removed,
leaves roughly chopped**

**1 bunch rainbow chard, stalks
removed, leaves roughly chopped**

**1 bunch English spinach, trimmed,
leaves roughly chopped**

**300 g salmon fillet, skin and bones
removed, cut into cubes**

**400 g cauliflower, trimmed,
stem and florets roughly chopped**

1 tablespoon lemon thyme leaves

coconut oil or olive oil cooking spray

1 lemon, cut into wedges

1 Preheat the oven to 200°C (180°C fan-forced).

2 Place the coconut milk, garlic and ⅓ cup water in a large, deep frying
pan over high heat and bring to the boil. Add the kale, chard and
spinach and stir constantly until the mixture comes back to the boil.
Remove the pan from the heat and stand, covered, for 5 minutes
to wilt the leaves. Season to taste and stir gently to combine.
Spoon the mixture into a 2 litre baking dish and top with the salmon.

3 Place the cauliflower and lemon thyme in a bowl, season to taste
and spray lightly with cooking spray. Toss until well combined.
Spread the mixture evenly over the salmon.

4 Bake for 30 minutes or until cooked and golden – a skewer inserted into
the cauliflower should come out easily. Rest in the dish for 5 minutes,
then serve warm with lemon wedges.

PALEO   DAIRY
FREE   GLUTEN
FREE   REFINED
SUGAR FREE

EDAMAME SOBA NOODLES *and* CRISPY SESAME TOFU

SERVES 4 — PREP 15 MINUTES / COOK 5 MINUTES / STAND 5 MINUTES —
TOTAL CALORIES 1360 / CALORIES PER SERVE 340

Ponzu is a Japanese sauce made from rice wine vinegar, bonito seaweed flakes and yuzu (a Japanese citrus fruit). Supermarket varieties often have added soy sauce. It makes a great marinade and dipping sauce. You can buy frozen edamame (soybeans) and soba noodles at larger supermarkets and Asian grocers.

200 g firm tofu, thickly sliced

180 g packet wok-ready
soba noodles

100 g frozen shelled edamame

boiling water, to cover

1 egg white

1 tablespoon rice flour

1 tablespoon sesame seeds

2 teaspoons coconut oil

100 g sugar snap peas,
halved on the diagonal

20 g snowpea shoot leaves

2 tablespoons ponzu sauce

1   Place the tofu on a double thickness of paper towel and pat dry. Season to taste on all sides.

2   Put the noodles and edamame in a large heatproof bowl. Cover with boiling water, then stand for 5 minutes or until the noodles separate easily. Drain. Divide among four bowls and set aside.

3   Meanwhile, place the egg white in a bowl and whisk until very frothy. Add the flour and sesame seeds and whisk until well combined and smooth. Season to taste.

4   Heat the oil in a large heavy-based non-stick frying pan over high heat. Add the tofu to the egg white mixture and toss to coat well. Carefully add the tofu to the hot pan and cook, turning occasionally, for 3 minutes or until heated through, crisp and golden on both sides.

5   Divide the tofu among the noodle bowls and top with the sugar snap peas and leaves. Drizzle with ponzu sauce and serve warm.

VEGETARIAN DAIRY FREE   GLUTEN FREE   REFINED SUGAR FREE

BROCCOLI *and* LAMB KOFTA *with* HERBY BEETROOT SALAD

SERVES 4 — PREP 30 MINUTES / CHILL 30 MINUTES / COOK 10 MINUTES —
TOTAL CALORIES 767 / CALORIES PER SERVE 192

Kofta are delicious little balls made of ground meat, veggies or cheese (paneer).
In this recipe, they're made from a tasty combo of lamb, spices and broccoli.
Double the mixture and freeze half of the cooked kofta for another meal.

1 cup broccoli florets

300 g lamb mince

1 egg yolk

2 teaspoons ground allspice

2 teaspoons ground cinnamon

2 garlic cloves, crushed

1 cup flat-leaf parsley leaves

1 cup small mint leaves

**1 bunch baby beetroot, peeled,
finely sliced into rounds**

1 long green chilli, finely sliced

⅓ cup pomegranate seeds

**1 lemon, cut into wedges
(optional)**

1 Place the broccoli in the bowl of a food processor and process until finely chopped. Add the mince, egg yolk, allspice, cinnamon and garlic and season to taste, then process until the mixture is smooth, well combined and slightly sticky.

2 Line a large baking tray with foil. With clean damp hands, roll 1 tablespoon measures of the lamb mixture into rounds (you should have enough mixture to make 16). Flatten the rounds slightly, then put them on the prepared tray and chill for 30 minutes to set firm.

3 Heat a chargrill pan over medium heat. Add the kofta and cook for 3 minutes each side or until golden and cooked through.

4 Meanwhile, place the parsley, mint, beetroot, chilli and pomegranate seeds in a bowl, season to taste and toss gently to combine.

5 Divide the beetroot salad among four plates or one serving platter and top with the kofta. Serve warm with lemon wedges if using.

PALEO   DAIRY FREE   GLUTEN FREE   REFINED SUGAR FREE   LUNCHBOX FRIENDLY

FRESH and ZINGY,
but will fill
the biggest of
appetites – plus
it just looks so
PRETTY.

STIR-FRIED BROCCOLI *and* CASHEW CHICKEN

SERVES 4 — PREP 15 MINUTES / COOK 5 MINUTES — TOTAL CALORIES 813 / CALORIES PER SERVE 203

Cook this fave takeout meal at home and save time, money and calories.

2 teaspoons coconut oil

300 g skinless chicken breast fillet, halved horizontally, finely sliced and seasoned

1 bunch Chinese broccoli, trimmed, cut into 5 cm lengths

1 bunch broccolini, trimmed, halved crossways

2 tablespoons teriyaki sauce

⅓ cup Chicken Stock (see page 331)

1 small iceberg lettuce, thickly sliced into large rounds

3 tablespoons raw cashews, roasted and chopped

1 long red chilli, finely sliced

1 Heat the oil in a large wok over high heat. Once melted, add the chicken and cook, tossing, for 3 minutes. Add the Chinese broccoli, broccolini, teriyaki sauce and stock and stir-fry for another 2 minutes or until the chicken is cooked and the sauce has reduced.

2 Divide the lettuce among four plates and top with the chicken stir-fry. Sprinkle with cashews and chilli and serve.

DAIRY FREE   FREEZER FRIENDLY

RAINBOW VEGETABLE *and* FISH RED CURRY

SERVES 4 — PREP 25 MINUTES / COOK 15 MINUTES — TOTAL CALORIES 806 / CALORIES PER SERVE 202

Thai takeout can be loaded with calories. This veggie-filled alternative is delicious, nutritious and on the table before you know it. You'll find daikon radish at larger supermarkets and Asian grocers.

500 g daikon, peeled

1 tablespoon red curry paste

1 × 165 ml tin light coconut milk

2 cups Chicken Stock (see page 331)

4 kaffir lime leaves, bruised

300 g butternut pumpkin, peeled, seeded and chopped

300 g firm white fish fillets, skin and bones removed, cut into 3 cm pieces

125 g baby corn, halved lengthways

1 bunch baby pak choy, trimmed, leaves separated

125 g cherry tomatoes, halved

2 spring onions, finely sliced on the diagonal

1 Using a vegetable peeler, peel long, thin lengths from the daikon, then very finely slice the daikon lengths into strips. Place in a bowl, cover with cold tap water and chill until required.

2 Place the curry paste, coconut milk, stock and lime leaves in a deep frying pan over medium heat. Bring to a simmer, stirring, and cook for 5 minutes.

3 Add the pumpkin and fish to the curry sauce and simmer for 5 minutes. Add the corn and pak choy and simmer, covered, for 2 minutes or until the fish and vegetables are just tender. Remove the pan from the heat and gently stir in the tomato.

4 Drain the daikon noodles and divide among four bowls. Spoon over the curry and sprinkle with spring onion. Serve warm.

DAIRY FREE   GLUTEN FREE   FREEZER FRIENDLY

KALE

Lightly spray trimmed kale leaves with oil and season to taste. Place on the hot chargrill section of the barbecue for 1 minute on each side or until charred and crisp.

PUMPKIN

Finely slice wedges of pumpkin, leaving skin on. Spray lightly with oil before chargrilling over medium heat until tender and golden.

LEMON AND LIME WEDGES

Cut lemons into wedges and limes in half. Chargrill on a hot barbecue, cut-side down, for 2 minutes each side or until caramelised.

BRUSSELS SPROUTS

Toss halved Brussels sprouts with a little olive oil and tamari (gluten-free soy sauce). Chargrill for a few minutes until just tender and crisp.

SALT + PEPPER ALMONDS

Toss whole raw almonds with sea salt flakes and freshly ground black pepper, then spray lightly with oil. Place on the barbecue flatplate for a few minutes until toasted.

COOKED RICE

Add your favourite cooked rice to a hot barbecue flatplate along with a drizzle of olive oil to prevent sticking. Carefully toss for a few minutes or until crisp and golden.

WHOLE SWEET POTATO

Add small whole sweet potatoes to the barbecue over low heat and close the hood. Barbecue for 20 minutes or until tender. Halve and top with your favourite fillings.

BROCCOLINI

Trim and toss broccolini with olive oil and lime juice. Chargrill for a few minutes until crisp and tender.

CHEESE

Make foil parcels of feta or ricotta, a little extra virgin olive oil and your favourite herbs, and season to taste. Barbecue for a few minutes until heated through and serve with vegetable sticks or crackers.

FRUIT SALAD

Chargrill slices of pineapple, mandarin segments, whole strawberries or halved stone fruit on your barbecue until caramelised and warmed through. Serve drizzled with a little honey and dollop of full-cream Greek yoghurt for a delicious, mess-free dessert.

TINNED BEANS

Drain your favourite tinned beans or chickpeas and toss in a selection of spices (try dried chilli flakes and cumin seeds). Add to a hot barbecue flatplate and carefully toss for a few minutes until crisp and golden.

MUSSELS

Add whole debearded mussels to the barbecue flatplate, drizzle with a little beer and wait for them to pop open before eating straight from the hot plate.

ROAST TANDOORI CAULIFLOWER
and KANGAROO

SERVES 4 — PREP 25 MINUTES / COOK 30 MINUTES / STAND 5 MINUTES —
TOTAL CALORIES 800 / CALORIES PER SERVE 200

Kangaroo has always been at the top of my list of red meat – it's sustainable, nutritious and naturally low in fat. It's served here with tandoori-roasted cauliflower – magnificent!

2 tablespoons tandoori curry paste

1 quantity Creamy Dressing (see page 147)

1 cauliflower, trimmed, cut into 8 wedges

400 g kangaroo fillet, seasoned

½ cup mint leaves, roughly chopped

3 Lebanese cucumbers, finely sliced into rounds

1 bunch radishes, finely sliced into rounds

1 Preheat the oven to 200°C (180°C fan-forced). Line a large baking tray with baking paper.

2 Place the tandoori paste, half the dressing and 3 tablespoons water in a large bowl and season to taste. Mix well, then add the cauliflower and gently toss to coat.

3 Transfer the mixture to the prepared tray, making sure the cauliflower is in a single layer, and bake for 20 minutes. Add the kangaroo and bake for a further 10 minutes or until the cauliflower is tender and the kangaroo is cooked medium. Remove from the oven. Transfer the kangaroo to a heatproof board and rest for 5 minutes, then slice.

4 Place the mint, cucumber and radish in a bowl, season to taste and toss gently to combine. Divide among four plates and drizzle with the remaining dressing. Serve warm with the tandoori cauliflower and kangaroo fillet.

GLUTEN
FREE

The humble CAULI is the HERO here - just
watch the plates come back clean.

KIDS love to help put these together (plus they DEVOUR their hard work afterwards).

YAKITORI VEGETABLE *and* TOFU SKEWERS

SERVES 4 — PREP 30 MINUTES / COOK 10 MINUTES + COOLING — TOTAL CALORIES 596 / CALORIES PER SERVE 132

These are great to make for vegan friends when you're having a barbie. You'll find the fresh seaweed salad at fishmongers, big supermarkets or sushi bars, and sake and mirin at larger supermarkets and Asian grocers.

2 tablespoons sake

2 tablespoons mirin

3 tablespoons tamari (gluten-free soy sauce)

1 tablespoon pure maple syrup

2 cm piece of ginger, finely grated

150 g firm tofu, cut into 2 cm pieces

2 zucchini, thickly sliced

1 red capsicum, seeded and cut into 2 cm pieces

1 small white onion, cut into wedges

50 g fresh seaweed salad

100 g green cabbage, very finely shredded

1 Place the sake, mirin, tamari, maple syrup and ginger in a small saucepan over high heat. Bring to the boil, then reduce the heat to medium and simmer for 3 minutes or until slightly reduced and thickened. Remove the pan from the heat and cool the sauce to room temperature.

2 Line a baking tray with baking paper. Evenly thread the tofu, zucchini, capsicum and onion onto eight skewers. Transfer to the prepared tray and brush with half the sauce.

3 Place the seaweed salad and cabbage in a bowl and toss to combine. Chill until required.

4 Heat a large chargrill pan over medium heat. Add the skewers and cook, turning occasionally and basting with a little of the remaining sauce, for 5 minutes or until the vegetables are golden and just cooked.

5 Divide the seaweed salad mixture among four plates. Top with the skewers, drizzle with the remaining sauce and serve warm.

VEGAN VEGETARIAN   DAIRY FREE   GLUTEN FREE   REFINED SUGAR FREE

The BEST - enough said!

GREEN DHAL

SERVES 4 — PREP 15 MINUTES / COOK 25 MINUTES — TOTAL CALORIES 867 / CALORIES PER SERVE 267

Dhal, a staple food in India for millennia, is so simple, yet has the most exotic flavours.
The fresh curry leaves will soften during cooking, so eat them too.

1 onion

1 tablespoon coconut oil

⅓ cup small fresh curry leaves

2 teaspoons brown mustard seeds

½ teaspoon dried chilli flakes

2 teaspoons ground cumin

1 teaspoon ground turmeric

2 cm piece of ginger, finely grated

1 cup dried split red lentils

**1 litre Vegetable Stock
(see page 331)**

100 g baby spinach leaves

½ cup coriander leaves

1   Halve the onion. Thinly slice one half and finely chop the other half.

2   Heat half the oil in a large saucepan over high heat. Once melted, add the sliced onion and cook, stirring occasionally, for 3 minutes or until softened. Add the curry leaves, mustard seeds and chilli and cook, stirring occasionally, for a further 3 minutes or until the onion is deep golden and the spices are crisp. Using a slotted spoon, transfer the mixture to a heatproof bowl and set aside until required.

3   Heat the remaining oil in the same pan over high heat. Once melted, add the cumin, turmeric, ginger and chopped onion and cook, stirring, for 3 minutes or until the onion has softened and the spices are fragrant. Add the lentils and stock and bring to the boil, then reduce the heat to low and simmer gently, stirring occasionally, for 15 minutes or until the lentils are very soft and the stock has reduced. Remove the pan from the heat.

4   Add the spinach and half the coriander to the lentil mixture, season to taste and stir until well combined.

5   Divide the dhal among four bowls, spoon over the sliced onion mixture and sprinkle with the remaining coriander. Serve warm.

VEGAN
VEGETARIAN

DAIRY
FREE

GLUTEN
FREE

REFINED
SUGAR FREE

LUNCHBOX
FRIENDLY

FREEZER
FRIENDLY

FATTOUSH *with* SALMON

SERVES 4 — PREP 25 MINUTES / STAND 30 MINUTES / COOK 20 MINUTES + COOLING —
TOTAL CALORIES 1110 / CALORIES PER SERVE 278

Fattoush is an eastern Mediterranean dish said to have been created as a crafty way to
use up stale flatbread. But boy is it delicious! Don't forget the sumac for the extra zingy
citrus flavour.

**1 large wholemeal Lebanese bread,
split in half**

extra virgin olive oil cooking spray

2 teaspoons sumac

1 tablespoon extra virgin olive oil

**finely grated zest and juice
of 1 lemon**

1 garlic clove, crushed

**4 vine-ripened tomatoes,
cut into wedges**

**300 g salmon fillet, skin on,
bones removed**

**2 Lebanese cucumbers,
halved lengthways, finely sliced
on the diagonal**

1 small red onion, finely sliced

50 g baby rocket leaves

1 Preheat the oven to 180°C (160°C fan-forced) and line a large baking
tray with baking paper.

2 Place the bread on the prepared tray. Spray lightly with cooking spray
on both sides and sprinkle with half the sumac. Bake for 10 minutes
or until golden and crisp. Remove from the oven and cool on the tray.
Season with salt and break into large pieces.

3 Meanwhile, place the oil, lemon zest and juice, garlic, tomato and
remaining sumac in a large bowl. Season to taste and toss well to
combine. Stand, at room temperature and tossing occasionally, for
30 minutes or until the tomato releases all of its natural juices.

4 Preheat a grill to high. Line a baking tray with foil and spray lightly
with cooking spray. Carefully pull the skin away from the salmon and
pat dry with paper towel. Place the skin on the prepared tray, shiny-side
up and season to taste. Grill, turning occasionally, for 5 minutes or until
crisp and golden. Transfer to a heatproof chopping board, allow to cool,
then roughly chop.

5 Place the salmon fillet on the same tray and season to taste.
Grill for 1 minute each side for medium–rare or until cooked to
your liking. Transfer to heatproof board, rest for 5 minutes, then
cut into bite-sized pieces.

6 Add the cucumber, onion, rocket and flatbread to the tomato mixture
and toss gently to combine. Divide among four plates, top with the
salmon and sprinkle with the crispy salmon skin. Serve warm.

DAIRY
FREE

REFINED
SUGAR FREE

GOLDEN TAGINE

SERVES 4 — PREP 20 MINUTES / COOK 20 MINUTES — TOTAL CALORIES 1204 / CALORIES PER SERVE 301

A perfect midweek dinner, on the table in just over half an hour.

1 tablespoon extra virgin olive oil

1 small red onion, finely sliced

2 tomatoes, chopped

1 tablespoon tomato paste

½ teaspoon saffron threads

1 teaspoon cumin seeds

¼ teaspoon ground cinnamon

2 garlic cloves, sliced

2 baby fennel bulbs, finely sliced

500 g firm white fish fillets, skin and bones removed, cut into 4 cm pieces

finely grated zest and juice of 1 large lemon

1 × 400 g tin chickpeas, drained and rinsed

½ cup flat-leaf parsley, finely chopped

1 Heat the oil in a deep frying pan over high heat. Add the onion, tomato, tomato paste, saffron, cumin, cinnamon and garlic and cook, stirring, for 3 minutes or until the onion has softened. Add ½ cup water and bring to the boil. Boil for 2 minutes, then transfer half the sauce to a heatproof bowl.

2 Layer the fennel and fish over the sauce in the pan. Spoon over the remaining sauce in the bowl and sprinkle with the lemon zest and juice. Season to taste.

3 Cover with a tight-fitting lid and reduce the heat to low. Bring to a gentle simmer and cook for 15 minutes or until the fish is just tender.

4 Combine the chickpeas and parsley in a bowl, then divide among four plates. Spoon over the fish tagine and serve.

DAIRY FREE | GLUTEN FREE | REFINED SUGAR FREE | FREEZER FRIENDLY

LENTIL-NAISE MARINARA PARCELS

SERVES 4 — PREP 30 MINUTES / COOK 25 MINUTES + 5 MINUTES RESTING —
TOTAL CALORIES 1633 / CALORIES PER SERVE 408

Here's a totally different way to serve marinara – especially fun to serve
to dinner guests. Who doesn't love opening presents?

**2 cups Tomato Passata
(see page 330)**

**1 tablespoon tomato paste
with herbs and garlic**

400 g raw seafood marinara mix

**1 × 400 g tin brown lentils,
drained and rinsed**

2 spring onions, finely sliced

50 g mixed salad leaves

1 cup flat-leaf parsley leaves

1 carrot, peeled into ribbons

**1 green capsicum, seeded
and finely sliced**

**1 quantity Italian Dressing
(see page 146)**

1 Preheat the oven to 200°C (180°C fan-forced).

2 Place the passata, tomato paste, marinara mix, lentils and spring
onion in a large bowl, season to taste and mix until well combined.
Lay four large pieces of foil on a work surface, then top with large
pieces of baking paper. Spoon the marinara mixture evenly into the
centre of each piece of baking paper, then fold over the paper and foil
to firmly enclose the filling.

3 Place marinara parcels on a large baking tray and bake for 25 minutes
or until the seafood is just cooked. Remove from the oven and leave,
untouched, for 5 minutes.

4 Combine the salad leaves, parsley, carrot, capsicum and dressing in
a bowl. Season to taste and gently toss.

5 Remove the foil and place the paper parcels on serving plates, with the
salad alongside. Break the top of each parcel open and serve warm.

DAIRY FREE	GLUTEN FREE	REFINED SUGAR FREE	FREEZER FRIENDLY

Simply cook or just toss the following 'pasta' ideas
through these simple grab-and-go sauces
for super-simple midweek meal options.

1 TOMATO, GARLIC, CHILLI + ROCKET

Cook gluten-free fettuccine
in boiling water for 8
minutes or until just tender.
Drain, then toss with extra
virgin olive oil, finely sliced
garlic, dried chilli flakes,
baby rocket leaves and
chopped tomato.

2 CANNELLINI BEANS, OLIVES + SEMI-DRIED TOMATO

Spiralise raw zucchini into
a bowl to make spaghetti,
then toss with drained and
rinsed tinned cannellini
beans, baby black olives,
small basil leaves and
semi-dried tomatoes.

3 WATERCRESS, BROCCOLI, TUNA + LEMON

Soak rice noodles in boiling
water for 5 minutes until
just tender. Drain, then
toss with drained and
flaked tinned tuna in
springwater, finely grated
lemon zest, fresh lemon
juice, watercress leaves and
chopped raw broccoli florets.

4 RICOTTA, PARMESAN + CHIVES

Use your vegetable peeler to peel long, thin lengths from the carrot. Place the carrot pappardelle in a bowl and toss with crumbled fresh full-cream ricotta, finely grated parmesan and chopped chives.

5 PESTO, EGGPLANT + WALNUTS

Cook wholemeal spelt penne in boiling water for 10 minutes or until just tender. Drain, then toss with pesto (preferably homemade), sliced chargrilled eggplant and chopped walnuts.

6 CHICKEN, FETA + SPINACH

Cook macaroni in boiling water for 8 minutes or until just tender. Drain, then toss with chopped cooked chicken, sliced spring onion, crumbled Danish feta and baby spinach leaves.

VEGETABLE SPAGHETTI *with* BAKED MEATBALLS

SERVES 4 — PREP 35 MINUTES / COOK 25 MINUTES + 5 MINUTES RESTING —
TOTAL CALORIES 1549 / CALORIES PER SERVE 387

Spiralisers are cheap to buy and so simple to use – much quicker than cooking pasta
and you get way more nutrients and fewer calories. This is another meatball recipe
where you can cook extra for the freezer.

300 g beef mince

1 garlic clove, crushed

1 teaspoon mixed dried herbs

**1 litre Tomato Passata
(see page 330)**

extra virgin olive oil cooking spray

8 baby bocconcini, torn

4 zucchini, spiralised

4 carrots, spiralised

½ cup small basil leaves

1 Preheat the oven to 200°C (220°C fan-forced).

2 Place the mince, garlic and dried herbs in a bowl, season to taste and
mix until well combined. Form the mixture into eight firm meatballs.

3 Pour the passata into a 30 cm × 20 cm baking dish. Sit the meatballs
in the passata and lightly spray the tops with cooking spray. Bake for
25 minutes or until the meatballs are cooked and golden – when a
skewer is inserted in the centre the juices should run clear. Remove
from the oven and immediately top with bocconcini. Stand for 5 minutes.

4 Divide the spiralised zucchini and carrot among four bowls and season
to taste. Spoon over the meatball mixture, sprinkle with basil leaves
and serve warm.

GLUTEN
FREE

REFINED
SUGAR FREE

FREEZER
FRIENDLY

A great FAMILY all-rounder and GLUTEN-FREE to boot.

EGGPLANT, CAULIFLOWER *and* KANGAROO MOUSSAKA

SERVES 6 — PREP 30 MINUTES / COOK 30 MINUTES — TOTAL CALORIES 1330 / CALORIES PER SERVE 222

Nutritional yeast is made from tiny fungi grown on molasses, which are then dried and deactivated. It's a super-important source of protein and vitamins for vegans and tastes a lot like parmesan. (So, if you don't have any, just replace with grated parmesan.)

extra virgin olive oil cooking spray

1 eggplant, finely sliced into rounds

300 g kangaroo mince

1 red onion, finely chopped

1 carrot, finely chopped

1 zucchini, finely chopped

1 red capsicum, seeded and finely chopped

2 teaspoons dried oregano

1 teaspoon ground cinnamon

2 garlic cloves, crushed

1 litre Tomato Passata (see page 330)

2 tablespoons micro herbs (optional)

CAULIFLOWER 'CHEESE'

600 g cauliflower, trimmed, stems chopped, florets separated

1 tablespoon nutritional yeast

½ cup unsweetened almond milk, warmed

2 teaspoons extra virgin olive oil

1 tablespoon lemon juice

2 tablespoons finely sliced chives

1 Preheat a large chargrill pan over high heat. Lightly spray both sides of the eggplant slices with cooking spray and season to taste. Add half the eggplant to the chargrill and cook, turning occasionally, for 3 minutes or until just tender and golden. Remove and repeat with the remaining eggplant, then set aside until needed.

2 Heat a large saucepan over high heat, add the mince and onion and cook, stirring occasionally, for 5 minutes or until cooked and golden. Add the carrot, zucchini, capsicum, oregano, cinnamon, garlic and passata and bring to the boil. Reduce the heat to medium and simmer, stirring occasionally, for 15 minutes or until the vegetables are just tender and the sauce has reduced slightly. Season to taste.

3 Meanwhile, to make the cauliflower 'cheese', steam the cauliflower for 15 minutes or until tender. Transfer to a high-speed upright blender. Add all the remaining ingredients and season to taste, then blend until smooth and well combined.

4 Preheat a grill to medium–high.

5 Spoon the mince mixture into a 30 cm × 20 cm deep baking dish, top with the eggplant and then spoon over the cauliflower 'cheese'. Grill for 3 minutes or until golden and bubbling. Sprinkle with micro herbs and serve.

PALEO   DAIRY FREE   GLUTEN FREE   REFINED SUGAR FREE   LUNCHBOX FRIENDLY   FREEZER FRIENDLY

This cauliflower cheese topping
is BEYOND delicious

FRESH FOUR BEAN NACHOS

SERVES 4 — PREP 25 MINUTES — TOTAL CALORIES 985 / CALORIES PER SERVE 246

A nutritious, no-cook recipe with plenty of protein. Try to find a taco sauce with no
added sugar. You'll need a mandoline (or a very sharp knife and a lot of patience)
to finely slice your beetroot and sweet potato.

50 g fresh full-cream ricotta

1 small avocado, flesh chopped

finely grated zest and juice of 1 lime

**1 × 400 g tin four bean mix,
drained and rinsed**

2 celery stalks, finely chopped

2 zucchini

200 g mild taco sauce

1 beetroot, very finely sliced

**200 g sweet potato,
very finely sliced**

½ cup coriander leaves

1 Place the ricotta, avocado and lime zest and juice in the bowl of a small
food processor. Season to taste and process until smooth.

2 Finely chop one zucchini and slice the other very finely.

3 Place the bean mix, celery, chopped zucchini and taco sauce in a bowl.
Season to taste and stir until well combined.

4 Divide the beetroot, sweet potato and sliced zucchini among four plates.
Spoon the bean mixture over the top, followed by the avocado mixture.
Sprinkle with coriander and serve.

VEGETARIAN   GLUTEN FREE   REFINED SUGAR FREE   LUNCHBOX FRIENDLY

Inspired by my Paella COOK-OFF comps with my bestie – I think this might be the WINNER!

MUSSEL *and* CAULIFLOWER PAELLA

SERVES 4 — PREP 20 MINUTES / COOK 30 MINUTES / STAND 3 MINUTES —
TOTAL CALORIES 989 / CALORIES PER SERVE 158

An impressive dish you can serve up to guests without having to
spend half the day in the kitchen. Yum!

1 cauliflower, trimmed, stems chopped, florets separated

50 g cured chorizo, finely chopped

1 onion, finely chopped

2 teaspoons smoked paprika

large pinch of saffron threads

250 g cherry tomatoes, halved

2 cups Chicken Stock (see page 331)

1 small green capsicum, seeded and cut into strips

500 g cleaned black mussels

1 lemon, cut into wedges

1 Place the cauliflower stems in the bowl of a food processor and process until finely chopped (resembling rice). Transfer to a bowl. Repeat the process with the florets.

2 Place a large (30 cm) deep frying pan or paella pan over medium heat, add the chorizo and onion and cook, stirring occasionally, for 5 minutes or until light golden. Add the paprika, saffron and tomatoes and cook, stirring occasionally, for 5 minutes or until the tomatoes collapse.

3 Add the cauliflower rice to the tomato mixture and stir until well combined. Pour in the stock and stir, then bring to a simmer and cook for 8 minutes.

4 Scatter the capsicum over the cauliflower rice and add the mussels, pushing them halfway into the mixture. Simmer for 5 minutes or until the mussels have opened and the stock has reduced. Discard any mussels that don't open. Remove the pan from the heat and stand for 3 minutes. Season to taste and serve warm with lemon wedges.

PALEO · DAIRY FREE · GLUTEN FREE · REFINED SUGAR FREE

VEGETABLE LASAGNE

SERVES 6 — PREP 25 MINUTES / COOK 45 MINUTES — TOTAL CALORIES 1831 / CALORIES PER SERVE 305

One to make at the weekend and pop into the freezer to enjoy on busy weeknights.

1 litre Tomato Passata
(see page 330)

4 (185 g) small fresh lasagne sheets

4 zucchini, finely sliced lengthways

400 g butternut pumpkin, peeled,
seeded and finely sliced

1 bunch English spinach,
leaves removed

300 g fresh full-cream ricotta

2 egg whites, whisked

2 roma tomatoes, finely sliced

1 tablespoon lemon thyme leaves

2 tablespoons finely grated
vintage cheddar

1 Preheat the oven to 180°C (160°C fan-forced).

2 Spread 1 cup of the passata evenly over the base of a 30 cm × 18 cm baking dish. Layer with half the lasagne sheets, 1 cup passata, the zucchini and pumpkin, 1 more cup passata, the remaining pasta sheets, spinach leaves and finally the remaining passata.

3 Place the ricotta and egg white in a bowl and season to taste. Using a hand-held mixer, mix until well combined and smooth. Spoon the mixture evenly over the final layer of passata, top with sliced tomato and sprinkle over the thyme and cheese.

4 Bake for 45 minutes or until the pasta and vegetables are cooked – a skewer inserted in the centre should come out easily. Stand in the dish for 5 minutes, then serve.

VEGETARIAN

REFINED
SUGAR FREE

FREEZER
FRIENDLY

MEXICAN BLACK BEANS

SERVES 4 — PREP 20 MINUTES / STAND 25 MINUTES / COOK 10 MINUTES —
TOTAL CALORIES 1267 / CALORIES PER SERVE 317

Super-simple midweek Mexican.

2 tomatoes finely chopped

1 small red onion, finely chopped

1 small green capsicum, seeded
and finely chopped

1 corn cob, kernels removed

1 small red chilli, finely chopped

1 × 400 g tin black beans,
drained and rinsed

juice of 1 lime

½ cup coriander leaves

400 g beef rump steak

coconut oil or olive oil cooking spray

2 teaspoons Mexican spice
seasoning

1   Place the tomato, onion, capsicum, corn, chilli, beans, lime juice
    and coriander in a bowl. Season to taste and stir until well combined.
    Stand, stirring occasionally, at room temperature for 20 minutes.

2   Heat a large heavy-based non-stick frying pan over medium–high heat.
    Spray the beef lightly on both sides with cooking spray and sprinkle
    evenly with the spice seasoning. Pan-fry for 3 minutes each side for
    medium or until cooked to your liking. Transfer to a heatproof board
    and rest for 5 minutes, then finely slice.

3   Divide the beans among four plates, top with the steak and serve.

DAIRY
FREE

GLUTEN
FREE

REFINED
SUGAR FREE

SUPER-FAST vegetarian
meal - an all-out
GREEN WINNER.

GREEN ALFREDO FETTUCCINE

SERVES 4 — PREP 15 MINUTES / COOK 10 MINUTES — TOTAL CALORIES 885 / CALORIES PER SERVE 221

Alfredo is named after the Italian bloke who invented it, but it basically means pasta coated in parmesan cheese and butter. I've used yoghurt instead of butter, but the end result is just as creamy and delicious.

100 g dried fettuccine,
broken in half

250 g broccolini, trimmed,
cut into 5 cm lengths

150 g asparagus, trimmed,
halved crossways

100 g baby spinach leaves

½ cup full-cream Greek yoghurt

2 tablespoons finely
grated parmesan

1 garlic clove, chopped

2 tablespoons oregano leaves

2 tablespoons finely sliced chives

1 tablespoon pine nuts, roasted

1 Bring a large saucepan of water to the boil over high heat. Add the fettuccine and boil, stirring occasionally, for 6 minutes. Add the broccolini and asparagus and boil for a further 2 minutes or until the pasta and vegetables are just tender. Drain, reserving ½ cup of the cooking liquid. Return the pasta mixture to the pan, off the heat.

2 Place the spinach, yoghurt, parmesan, garlic and reserved cooking liquid in an upright blender and blend until smooth. Season to taste, then add to the pasta mixture and toss until well combined.

3 Mix together the oregano, chives and pine nuts in a bowl and season to taste.

4 Divide the pasta mixture among four bowls. Top with the pine nut mixture and serve.

VEGETARIAN   REFINED
SUGAR FREE   LUNCHBOX
FRIENDLY

SALT *and* PEPPER BARBECUED CAULIFLOWER *with* PRAWNS

SERVES 4 — PREP 25 MINUTES / COOK 15 MINUTES — TOTAL CALORIES 519 / CALORIES PER SERVE 130

I don't know why food barbecued outdoors tastes better – perhaps because the light
and air elevates our mood. Whatever the reason, this is another chargrilled delight
that won't disappoint.

1 cauliflower, trimmed, stems
sliced, florets removed and halved

coconut oil or olive oil cooking spray

2 teaspoons sea salt flakes

2 teaspoons freshly ground
black pepper

1 red onion, sliced into rings

3 tablespoons pomegranate seeds

2 tablespoons dill fronds

16 raw king prawns, peeled
and deveined, tails intact

2 limes, halved

mixed green salad leaves, to serve

1 Heat a large barbecue chargrill pan over medium–high heat.

2 Place the cauliflower in a large heatproof bowl. Spray lightly with
cooking spray, season with the salt and pepper and toss to coat.
Chargrill, turning occasionally, for 5 minutes or until just tender.
Return to the bowl.

3 Chargrill the onion, turning once, for 3 minutes or until just tender
and golden. Transfer to the bowl with the cauliflower, then add the
pomegranate and dill fronds and gently toss to combine. Set aside
until required.

4 Thread the prawns onto eight skewers. Spray lightly with cooking spray
and season to taste. Place the skewers and lime halves, cut-side down,
on the chargrill and cook, turning the skewers once, for 4 minutes or
until the prawns are just cooked and golden.

5 Divide the cauliflower mixture among four plates, add the skewers
and lime halves and serve warm with salad leaves.

PALEO   DAIRY FREE   GLUTEN FREE   REFINED SUGAR FREE

Snacks

Be sure to PORTION-CONTROL these bad boys - they're SOOOOO good.

CACAO CHILLI NUTS

SERVES 6 — PREP 10 MINUTES / COOK 15 MINUTES + COOLING —
TOTAL CALORIES 1175 / CALORIES PER SERVE 196

This is the kind of snack that suits growing teenagers or blokes who are training hard.
If you are trying to keep your weight down, and you know you won't be able to stop at
one or two nuts, maybe try something less calorie-dense.

1 egg white

3 teaspoons pure maple syrup

**1 teaspoon raw cacao powder
(see page 296)**

¼ teaspoon ground cinnamon

½ teaspoon chilli powder

1 cup blanched almonds

½ cup raw cashews

**2 medjool dates, pitted
and finely chopped**

1 Preheat the oven to 200°C (180°C fan-forced) and line a large baking
   tray with baking paper.

2 Place the egg white in a large bowl and whisk until frothy. Add the
   maple syrup, cacao, cinnamon and chilli and whisk until well combined.
   Add the almonds and cashews and toss together.

3 Spread the mixture in a single layer on the prepared tray and bake for
   15 minutes or until the nuts are golden and crisp. Cool on the tray.

4 Add the dates to the nut mixture and toss to combine. Serve.

VEGETARIAN PALEO DAIRY FREE GLUTEN FREE REFINED SUGAR FREE LUNCHBOX FRIENDLY

AVO SMASH *with* BEETROOT

SERVES 4 — PREP 15 MINUTES — TOTAL CALORIES 254 / CALORIES PER SERVE 64

These make gorgeous party snacks. If you want to put them in lunchboxes, press two together to make little sandwiches. You'll need an Asian vegetable slicer or mandoline to cut the beetroot into very thin (2 mm) slices.

1 small avocado, flesh chopped

finely grated zest and juice of 1 lime

1 celery stalk, finely chopped

1 spring onion, finely sliced

1 beetroot, very finely sliced

micro herbs (optional) and 1 lime, extra, cut into wedges, to serve

1 Place the avocado and lime zest and juice in a bowl and season to taste. Using a fork, mash together until well combined. Stir in the celery and spring onion.

2 Spoon the avocado smash on top of the beetroot slices. Sprinkle with micro herbs, season again if you like, and serve with extra lime wedges.

 VEGAN VEGETARIAN PALEO DAIRY FREE GLUTEN FREE REFINED SUGAR FREE LUNCHBOX FRIENDLY

PARTY TIME!

FILLING and MOREISH.
Great for lunchboxes or
a grab-and-go snack.

BAKED HERB RICOTTA

MAKES 20 — PREP 15 MINUTES / COOK 20 MINUTES + COOLING —
TOTAL CALORIES 748 / CALORIES PER SERVE 37

Simple little snacks that the kids (and grown-ups) will love.

extra virgin olive oil cooking spray

400 g fresh full-cream ricotta

2 eggs, whisked

1 tablespoon finely grated
parmesan

1 tablespoon finely sliced chives

1¼ tablespoons thyme leaves

10 small cherry tomatoes, halved

1 Preheat the oven to 200° (180°C fan-forced). Lightly spray 20 holes
   of a 24-hole mini muffin tin with cooking spray.

2 Place the ricotta, egg, parmesan, chives and 1 tablespoon thyme
   in a bowl and season to taste. Stir until well combined and smooth.
   Spoon the mixture evenly into the prepared muffin holes.

3 Gently press a tomato half on top of each one, with the cut side facing
   up. Spray lightly with cooking spray, season to taste and sprinkle with
   the remaining thyme.

4 Bake for 20 minutes or until set firm and golden. Cool for 10 minutes
   in the tin, then serve warm.

VEGETARIAN   GLUTEN   REFINED   LUNCHBOX   FREEZER
              FREE   SUGAR FREE   FRIENDLY   FRIENDLY

FRESH TRAIL MIX

MAKES 6 CUPS {SERVES 12} — PREP 10 MINUTES/ CHILL 1 HOUR — TOTAL CALORIES 481 / CALORIES PER SERVE 40

This is a trail mix like no other. If you want to take some on a walk, pop it in zip-lock bag inside a lunch-bag cooler so it stays nice and cold.

2 carrots, quartered lengthways, finely sliced on the diagonal

1 zucchini, quartered lengthways, finely sliced

2 celery stalks, finely sliced

3 tablespoons sunflower seeds

125 g blueberries

8 seedless red grapes, halved lengthways

1 teaspoon finely grated lemon zest

1 tablespoon lemon juice

½ teaspoon fennel seeds

1 Place all the ingredients in a bowl and toss until well combined. Chill for 1 hour. Serve chilled.

VEGAN VEGETARIAN

PALEO

DAIRY FREE

GLUTEN FREE

REFINED SUGAR FREE

LUNCHBOX FRIENDLY

DRIED TRAIL MIX

MAKES ABOUT 2 CUPS (SERVES 8) — PREP 10 MINUTES — TOTAL CALORIES 1152 / CALORIES PER SERVE 189

An amazing energy-booster. Puffed quinoa is available from health-food shops.

3 tablespoons flaked almonds

3 tablespoons walnut halves, chopped

½ cup pumpkin seeds

½ cup puffed quinoa

3 tablespoons pecans, chopped

⅓ cup craisins

¼ teaspoon freshly grated nutmeg

1   Place all the ingredients in a bowl and toss until well combined. Serve.

VEGAN VEGETARIAN   PALEO   DAIRY FREE   GLUTEN FREE   LUNCHBOX FRIENDLY

SPICED TAMARI EDAMAME

SERVES 4 — PREP 5 MINUTES / COOK 5 MINUTES — TOTAL CALORIES 532 / CALORIES PER SERVE 133

Edamame (soybeans) are one of my favourite snacks, and the spice mix in this recipe just takes them up a notch. Look for them in the freezer section of larger supermarkets and Asian grocers.

2 teaspoons coconut oil

2 teaspoons cumin seeds

2 teaspoons coriander seeds

1 teaspoon dried chilli flakes

300 g frozen edamame pods

2 tablespoons tamari
(gluten-free soy sauce)

1   Heat the oil in a wok over high heat. Once melted, add the cumin, coriander and chilli and cook, tossing, for 1 minute or until fragrant and crisp.

2   Add the edamame and tamari and toss for 2 minutes or until the edamame are well coated in the spice mix and heated through. Serve warm.

VEGAN
VEGETARIAN   DAIRY
FREE   GLUTEN
FREE   REFINED
SUGAR FREE   LUNCHBOX
FRIENDLY

GREEN GOODNESS SOUP

SERVES 6 — PREP 15 MINUTES / COOK 15 MINUTES — TOTAL CALORIES 798 / CALORIES PER SERVE 133

Blending lettuce in soup may sound a bit 70s, but trust me – it adds
an amazing sweetness. This super-low-calorie soup is delicious served
warm or chilled, making it perfect for lunchtime leftovers.

4 spring onions, finely sliced

**2 celery stalks, pale inner leaves
reserved, finely sliced**

2 garlic cloves, crushed

1 long green chilli, sliced

**2 cups Vegetable Stock
(see page 331)**

100 g baby spinach leaves

20 g baby rocket leaves

1 butter lettuce, trimmed and sliced

1 Place the spring onion, celery, garlic, chilli and stock in a large
saucepan over medium heat. Bring to a simmer, then reduce the heat
to low and cook, covered and stirring occasionally, for 15 minutes or
until the celery is very tender.

2 Remove the pan from the heat and stir in the remaining ingredients.
Season to taste. Using a hand-held blender, blend until smooth.
Serve topped with the reserved celery leaves.

VEGAN
VEGETARIAN   PALEO   DAIRY
FREE   GLUTEN
FREE   REFINED
SUGAR FREE   LUNCHBOX
FRIENDLY

Green is GOOD.
green is GO!

PARMESAN VEGETABLE FRIES

SERVES 4 — PREP 15 MINUTES / COOK 30 MINUTES — TOTAL CALORIES 388 / CALORIES PER SERVE 97

Thinly cut parsnips make the most delicious oven-baked veggie chips because
they are naturally sweet. Here, the parmesan adds a salty, umami flavour

2 zucchini, cut into thick chips

2 parsnips, cut into thin chips

3 tablespoons finely grated parmesan

coconut oil or olive oil cooking spray

1 Preheat the oven to 220°C (200°C fan-forced) and line a large baking tray with baking paper.

2 Place the zucchini, parsnip and parmesan in a bowl and season to taste. Spray lightly with cooking spray, then toss well to combine. Arrange on the prepared tray in a single layer.

3 Bake for 30 minutes or until cooked, crisp and golden. Serve warm.

Anyone who knows me well knows I'm a DIEHARD CHIP FAN. These fries definitely hit the spot.

VEGETARIAN

GLUTEN FREE

REFINED SUGAR FREE

246

CAULIFLOWER *and* BROCCOLI POPCORN

SERVES 4 — PREP 15 MINUTES / COOK 30 MINUTES / STAND 5 MINUTES —
TOTAL CALORIES 236 / CALORIES PER SERVE 59

My healthy take on popcorn, perfect for chick-flick nights. You'll find all-purpose
seasoning in the supermarket – it's a mix of garlic, celery, onion, herbs and spices.

300 g small cauliflower florets

300 g small broccoli florets

coconut oil or olive oil cooking spray

2 teaspoons all-purpose seasoning

1 Preheat the oven to 200°C (180°C fan-forced). Line a large baking tray with baking paper.

2 Place the cauliflower and broccoli in a bowl and spray lightly with cooking spray. Add the seasoning and season to taste with salt and pepper, then gently toss together until well combined.

3 Spread out the mixture in a single layer on the prepared tray and bake, turning once, for 30 minutes or until tender, crisp and golden. Stand on the tray for 5 minutes, then serve warm.

VEGAN VEGETARIAN   PALEO   DAIRY FREE   GLUTEN FREE   REFINED SUGAR FREE

The same GREAT FLAVOURS as traditional sushi, but no messy rice and rolling.

ZUCCHINI SUSHI

SERVES 4 — PREP 20 MINUTES — TOTAL CALORIES 158 / CALORIES PER SERVE 40

To make your long, flat zucchini strips, use a vegetable peeler or a mandoline.

2 tablespoons tamari
(gluten-free soy sauce)

1 cm piece of ginger, finely grated

1 small red chilli, finely chopped

2 large zucchini, peeled into
long strips

½ cup bean sprouts

1 small carrot, cut into matchsticks

1 small Lebanese cucumber,
cut into matchsticks

1 Place the tamari, ginger and chilli in a bowl and stir until well combined. Set aside until required.

2 Lay strips of zucchini out flat on a clean work surface. At one short end of each zucchini strip, place some bean sprouts, carrot and cucumber. Roll up tightly to enclose the filling.

3 Divide among four plates and serve with the tamari mixture alongside.

VEGAN
VEGETARIAN

DAIRY
FREE

GLUTEN
FREE

REFINED
SUGAR FREE

LUNCHBOX
FRIENDLY

TOPPED PAPPADAMS

SERVES 4 — PREP 10 MINUTES / COOK 2 MINUTES — TOTAL CALORIES 198 / CALORIES PER SERVE 50

Another simple, satisfying yet low-cal recipe for your next dinner party!

12 mini pappadams

2 tablespoons finely chopped mint

1 tablespoon full-cream Greek yoghurt

1 Lebanese cucumber, finely sliced into rounds

3 tablespoons small coriander leaves

½ teaspoon celery seeds

1 Microwave the pappadams, in batches, on high for 1 minute or until puffed, crisp and light golden. Cool.

2 Place the mint and yoghurt in a bowl, season to taste and stir until well combined.

3 Top the pappadams with the cucumber, then the mint and yoghurt mixture and coriander leaves. Sprinkle with celery seeds and serve.

VEGETARIAN   REFINED SUGAR FREE

TUNA *and* WILD RICE SLICE

SERVES 8 — PREP 15 MINUTES / COOK 40 MINUTES + COOLING —
TOTAL CALORIES 1042 / CALORIES PER SERVE 130

Wild rice is a great source of antioxidants. This lunchbox-friendly slice couldn't
be easier to make.

1 × 195 g tin tuna in springwater, drained and flaked

1 cup cooked wild rice (from ½ cup uncooked rice)

4 eggs, whisked

2 zucchini, finely chopped

50 g baby spinach leaves, chopped

½ cup wholemeal plain flour

2 tablespoons finely grated parmesan

1 Preheat the oven to 180°C (160°C fan-forced). Line the base and sides of a 28 cm × 18 cm baking tin with baking paper.

2 Place all the ingredients in a bowl, season to taste and mix until well combined. Spoon the mixture into the prepared pan and level the surface.

3 Bake for 40 minutes or until golden and a skewer inserted in the centre comes out clean. Cool completely in the tin. Cut into eight pieces and serve.

LUNCHBOX FRIENDLY

REFINED SUGAR FREE

FREEZER FRIENDLY

COTTAGE CHEESE LETTUCE WRAPS

SERVES 4 — PREP 15 MINUTES — TOTAL CALORIES 116 / CALORIES PER SERVE 29

Super-low-calorie snack.

½ cup cottage cheese

1 long red chilli, finely chopped

2 tablespoons finely chopped basil

8 small inner iceberg lettuce leaves

1 lemon, cut into wedges

1 Place the cottage cheese, chilli and basil in a bowl. Season to taste and stir until well combined.

2 Spoon the mixture into the lettuce leaves and roll up. Serve the lemon wedges alongside.

VEGETARIAN GLUTEN FREE REFINED SUGAR FREE

The FASTEST snack on the block.

SESAME CUCUMBER 'NUGGETS'

SERVES 4 — PREP 5 MINUTES — TOTAL CALORIES 218 / CALORIES PER SERVE 55

Brilliantly simple, yet you're getting vitamins, antioxidants,
minerals and fibre with minimal calories.

**2 tablespoons sesame
seeds, roasted**

**2 teaspoons lemon
pepper seasoning**

**4 Lebanese cucumbers,
halved lengthways,
then cut into 3 cm pieces**

1 Place the sesame seeds and lemon pepper seasoning in a bowl and
   stir to combine

2 Press the cut sides of the cucumber pieces into the sesame mixture
   and serve.

VEGAN
VEGETARIAN   PALEO   DAIRY
FREE   GLUTEN
FREE   REFINED
SUGAR FREE   LUNCHBOX
FRIENDLY

ZUCCHINI HUMMUS *with* CRACKERS

SERVES 6 — PREP 20 MINUTES — TOTAL CALORIES 1921 / CALORIES PER SERVE 324

This recipe makes 2 cups of hummus, which is 556 calories. The recipe
for the crackers is on page 260.

1 zucchini, chopped

1 × 400 g tin chickpeas,
drained and rinsed

1 garlic clove, peeled and left whole

1 tablespoon unhulled tahini

finely grated zest and juice
of 1 lemon

2 teaspoons avocado oil

¼ teaspoon sumac

1 bunch (about 7) radishes,
trimmed and halved

1 Lebanese cucumber,
cut into thick chips

1 carrot, cut into thick chips

½ quantity Curry Seeded Crackers
(see page 260)

1 Place the zucchini, chickpeas, garlic, tahini and lemon zest and juice in
the bowl of a food processor, season to taste and process until smooth
and well combined.

2 Transfer the hummus to a shallow serving bowl, then drizzle with
oil and sprinkle with sumac. Place the radish, cucumber, carrot and
crackers alongside and serve.

VEGAN
VEGETARIAN

DAIRY
FREE

GLUTEN
FREE

REFINED
SUGAR FREE

LUNCHBOX
FRIENDLY

CURRY SEEDED CRACKERS

SERVES 8 — PREP 5 MINUTES / STAND 20 MINUTES / COOK 1 HOUR + COOLING —
TOTAL CALORIES 2272 / CALORIES PER SERVE 290

These little gems of goodness are full of fibre, minerals and protein. Serve them with
zucchini hummus (see page 258) for an additional 46 calories per tablespoon.

1½ cups sunflower seeds

½ cup linseeds

½ cup sesame seeds

3 tablespoons chia seeds

3 teaspoons sea salt flakes

3 teaspoons curry powder

1 Place all the ingredients and 1½ cups warm water in a heatproof bowl
and stir until well combined. Leave to stand at room temperature,
stirring occasionally, for 20 minutes or until the mixture thickens and
looks gel-like.

2 Meanwhile, preheat the oven to 160°C (140°C fan-forced) and line two
large baking trays with baking paper.

3 Spread the seed mixture thinly and evenly over the prepared trays,
making sure there are no gaps. Bake for 1 hour, swapping the trays
halfway through baking, until crisp and light golden. Cool completely
on the trays, then snap into rough pieces to serve.

VEGAN
VEGETARIAN   PALEO   DAIRY   GLUTEN   REFINED   LUNCHBOX
                          FREE   FREE   SUGAR FREE   FRIENDLY

CAULIFLOWER DIP *with* CUMIN

SERVES 4 — PREP 10 MINUTES / COOK 10 MINUTES + COOLING —
TOTAL CALORIES 339 / CALORIES PER SERVE 85

One of my fave veggies with a touch of spice for added moreishness.

400 g cauliflower florets

2 tablespoons raw cashews

**½ cup Vegetable Stock
(see page 331)**

1 tablespoon fresh lime juice

1 cup flat-leaf parsley leaves

1 teaspoon cumin seeds, toasted

**2 bunches mixed baby carrots,
trimmed, skins scrubbed**

1 Place the cauliflower, cashews and stock in a saucepan over high heat. Bring to the boil, then reduce the heat to medium and simmer, covered and stirring occasionally, for 10 minutes or until the nuts and cauliflower are tender and the stock has reduced. Cool in the pan for 10 minutes.

2 Transfer the mixture to the bowl of a food processor. Add the lime juice and season to taste, then process until smooth and well combined. Stir in the parsley.

3 Spoon the dip into a serving bowl and sprinkle with the cumin seeds. Serve with the baby carrots for dipping.

VEGAN
VEGETARIAN PALEO DAIRY
FREE GLUTEN
FREE REFINED
SUGAR FREE LUNCHBOX
FRIENDLY

APPLE NUT BUTTER SANDWICHES

SERVES 4 — PREP 20 MINUTES — TOTAL CALORIES 463 / CALORIES PER SERVE 116

My nan always made me peanut butter and apple sandwiches.
This is a great low-cal alternative.

1 green apple, very finely sliced, seeded

1 red apple, very finely sliced, seeded

1 teaspoon finely grated lemon zest

2 tablespoons fresh lemon juice

3 tablespoons 100 per cent cashew spread

1 Place the apple slices, lemon zest and juice in a bowl and toss together until well combined.

2 Spread half the apple slices with the cashew spread. Sandwich with the remaining slices and serve.

VEGAN VEGETARIAN   PALEO   DAIRY FREE   GLUTEN FREE   REFINED SUGAR FREE

1 **Dip into** finely chopped mixed fresh herbs and dried chilli flakes.

3 **Sprinkle with** dukkah.

5 **Wrap in** English spinach, garnish with herbs and season.

2 **Serve with** sliced smoked salmon and garnish with fennel fronds.

4 **Top with** finely grated parmesan and herbs.

6 **Add** Japanese Dressing (see page 147) and toasted sesame seeds.

GRAB A BOILED
Egg

Soft-boil your eggs in gently rolling water for 3 minutes, then serve immediately with these delicious additions.

6

LUNCHBOX OAT SLICE

MAKES 12 PIECES — PREP 15 MINUTES / COOK 30 MINUTES / STAND 30 MINUTES —
TOTAL CALORIES 2626 / CALORIES PER SERVE 220

This is a brilliant occasional snack for the kids' lunchboxes, and you'll feel extra-good knowing exactly what you're feeding your little ones.

1½ cups quick oats

3 tablespoons pure maple syrup

100 g butter, melted

2 teaspoons vanilla bean paste or extract

½ cup craisins

1 cup pumpkin seeds

½ cup shredded coconut

1 egg, whisked

1 Preheat the oven to 180°C (160°C fan-forced). Line the base and sides of a 30 cm × 20 cm slice tin with baking paper.

2 Place all the ingredients in a bowl and stir until well combined. Transfer to the prepared tray and press down firmly, then level the surface. Bake for 30 minutes or until golden and set firm in the middle.

3 Stand in the tin for 30 minutes, then transfer the slice to a chopping board and cut into 12 pieces. The slice will keep well in an airtight container in the fridge for up to a week, or you can store individually wrapped portions in the freezer for up to 2 months.

VEGETARIAN   REFINED SUGAR FREE   LUNCHBOX FRIENDLY   FREEZER FRIENDLY

Adult AND kids' lunchboxes
will love these.

UM, YUM! These pack a SWEETNESS PUNCH to satisfy the sweetest of sweet tooths.

RAW JAM THUMBPRINT COOKIES

MAKES 17 — PREP 20 MINUTES / CHILL 1 HOUR — TOTAL CALORIES 1575 / CALORIES PER SERVE 88

Almonds are rich in protein, fibre and minerals, and even though they
are high in fat, it's mostly monounsaturated.

1 cup almond meal

½ cup 100 per cent almond spread

2 tablespoons pure maple syrup

**2 teaspoons vanilla bean paste
or extract**

**2 tablespoons Strawberry Chia Jam
(see page 89)**

1 Line a large baking tray with baking paper.

2 Place the almond meal, almond spread, maple syrup and vanilla
in a bowl and stir until well combined. Roll tablespoons of the mixture
into smooth balls and place on the prepared tray, about 4 cm apart.

3 Using the end of a wooden spoon, gently press the centre of each ball
to flatten it to a 3 cm round, leaving an indent (the edges will crack
slightly). Fill the indents with jam.

4 Chill for 1 hour or until firm. Serve chilled.

VEGAN VEGETARIAN

PALEO

DAIRY FREE

GLUTEN FREE

REFINED SUGAR FREE

LUNCHBOX FRIENDLY

MOCHA FRAPPE

SERVES 4 — PREP 10 MINUTES — TOTAL CALORIES 102 / CALORIES PER SERVE 26

Maca powder is made from the root of a South American plant, and is high in complex carbs, protein, minerals and dietary fibre. You'll find it in health-food shops.

1 cup freshly brewed coffee, cooled

2 teaspoons raw cacao powder (see page 296)

1 tablespoon maca powder

1 tablespoon pure maple syrup

3 tablespoons unsweetened almond milk

2 cups ice cubes

1 Place all the ingredients in a high-speed upright blender and blend until smooth.

2 Pour into four tall chilled glasses and serve immediately with a straw and a long spoon.

VEGAN VEGETARIAN PALEO DAIRY FREE GLUTEN FREE REFINED SUGAR FREE

RICOTTA WHIP

SERVES 4 — PREP 10 MINUTES — TOTAL CALORIES 354 / CALORIES PER SERVE 89

A simple little recipe to remind you that healthy eating
doesn't mean you have to go without.

50 g fresh full-cream ricotta

**2 tablespoons full-cream
Greek yoghurt**

2 teaspoons honey

**1 teaspoon vanilla bean paste
or extract**

**2 oranges, peeled, finely sliced
into rings**

125 g raspberries

1   Place the ricotta, yoghurt, honey and vanilla in a bowl.
Using a hand-held mixer, mix on high speed for 2 minutes
or until well combined and smooth.

2   Divide the orange slices and raspberries among four bowls,
top with the whipped ricotta and serve.

VEGETARIAN

GLUTEN
FREE

REFINED
SUGAR FREE

Make DOUBLE of these so you have a week of great GO-TO SNACKS.

OVEN-DRIED FRUIT

SERVES 4 — PREP 10 MINUTES / COOK 1 HOUR + COOLING — TOTAL CALORIES 318 / CALORIES PER SERVE 80

Great little lunchbox fillers. Adults can make a mini trail mix with a couple
of these and 5–6 nuts (nuts are about 7–10 calories each).

**300 g peeled, cored pineapple,
cut into thin 3 cm pieces**

**1 green apple, very finely
sliced, seeded**

**1 red apple, very finely
sliced, seeded**

1 Preheat the oven to 140°C (120°C fan-forced). Set wire racks over
two large baking trays, and line two separate baking trays with
baking paper.

2 Place the fruit in a single layer on the racks set over trays.
Bake, turning once, for 1 hour, or until crisp and light golden.
Immediately transfer the fruit from the racks to the lined trays
and leave to cool completely. Serve or store in an airtight container
in a cool dark place for up to 3 days.

VEGAN
VEGETARIAN   PALEO   DAIRY
FREE   GLUTEN
FREE   REFINED
SUGAR FREE   LUNCHBOX
FRIENDLY

ALMOND CHAI

SERVES 4 — PREP 10 MINUTES / COOK 10 MINUTES / STAND 20 MINUTES —
TOTAL CALORIES 615 / CALORIES PER SERVE 154

I'm a big chai fan. This really is a perfect mid-afternoon pick-me-up.

2 cinnamon sticks

2 dried bay leaves

8 cardamom pods, bruised

4 black peppercorns

8 cloves

2 cm piece of ginger, thickly sliced

2 English breakfast teabags

100 g blanched almonds

**1 teaspoon vanilla bean paste
or extract**

1½ teaspoons fennel seeds, roasted

1 Place the cinnamon sticks, bay leaves, cardamom pods, peppercorns, cloves, ginger, teabags and 1 litre water in a saucepan over high heat. Bring to the boil, then reduce the heat to low and simmer gently for 10 minutes. Strain the mixture into a heatproof bowl, reserving the cinnamon to use as a garnish if you like, and discarding the remaining flavourings.

2 Add the almonds and vanilla to the hot spiced water and stand, covered, for 20 minutes or until the almonds have softened.

3 Transfer the almond mixture to a high-speed upright blender and blend until smooth. Pour into serving glasses, top with a sprinkling of fennel seeds and serve warm.

VEGAN VEGETARIAN   PALEO   DAIRY FREE   GLUTEN FREE   REFINED SUGAR FREE

DECADENT HOT CHOCOLATE

SERVES 4 — PREP 10 MINUTES / COOK 5 MINUTES — TOTAL CALORIES 1133 / CALORIES PER SERVE 208

Ah, yes please!

100 g dark chocolate (70 per cent cocoa), chopped

2 tablespoons pure maple syrup

3 cups coconut almond milk

½ quantity Coco-cream (see page 302)

freshly grated nutmeg, to serve

1 Place the chocolate, maple syrup and milk in a saucepan over low heat. Cook, stirring, for 5 minutes or until smooth and well combined and the mixture just comes to a simmer.

2 Pour the mixture into four mugs or heatproof glasses, dollop with coco-cream and sprinkle with nutmeg. Serve warm with a spoon.

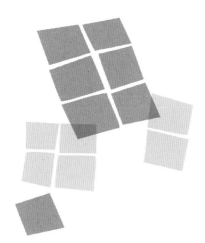

VEGETARIAN

GLUTEN FREE

SWEET TURMERIC MILK

Turmeric has wonderful anti-inflammatory qualities. If you've not
tried it in a warm drink before, I urge you to give this a go!

1 litre coconut almond milk

1 tablespoon pure maple syrup

2 teaspoons ground turmeric

1 teaspoon ground cinnamon

1 tablespoon shredded coconut

½ teaspoon freshly grated nutmeg

1 Place the milk, maple syrup, turmeric and cinnamon in a saucepan over medium heat. Bring to a simmer, stirring, then remove the pan from the heat.

2 Pour the milk mixture into four cups, top with the coconut and nutmeg and serve warm.

VEGAN VEGETARIAN   PALEO   DAIRY FREE   GLUTEN FREE   REFINED SUGAR FREE

Sweet Treats

HOMEMADE SUPERFOOD CHOCOLATES

MAKES 14 — PREP 10 MINUTES / CHILL 2 HOURS — TOTAL CALORIES 1250 / CALORIES PER SERVE 89

Buckinis are raw buckwheat groats that have been soaked then dried at a very low heat
to preserve their awesome nutrients. You'll find them in health-food stores and online.

2 tablespoons craisins

**1 tablespoon toasted buckinis
(buckwheat)**

1 tablespoon chia seeds

1 tablespoon shredded coconut

⅓ cup coconut oil, melted

**1 cup raw cacao powder
(see page 296)**

3 tablespoons pure maple syrup

**1 tablespoon vanilla bean paste
or extract**

1 Place the craisins, buckinis, chia seeds and shredded coconut in a bowl
and mix until well combined. Divide half the mixture among 14 holes
of a 2 tablespoon capacity ice-cube tray.

2 Place the coconut oil, cacao powder, maple syrup and vanilla in a
heatproof jug and whisk until well combined and smooth. Spoon evenly
over the craisin mixture in the tray, then sprinkle with the remaining
craisin mixture. Chill for 2 hours or until set firm. Serve chilled.

*It's HOMEMADE and it's
CHOCOLATE - enough said!*

VEGAN
VEGETARIAN   DAIRY
FREE   GLUTEN
FREE   REFINED
SUGAR FREE   FREEZER
FRIENDLY

I love a good LOLLY and these are DELICIOUS and OH-SO-GOOD.

CRANBERRY JELLY LOLLIES

MAKES 18 — PREP 5 MINUTES / COOK 5 MINUTES / STAND 5 MINUTES / CHILL 4 HOURS —
TOTAL CALORIES 208 / CALORIES PER SERVE 12

You can buy small silicon ice-cube moulds from department stores.
Or you could spoon the mixture into a 20 cm square cake tin lined with baking paper,
then cut into small pieces when set.

**⅔ cup cranberry juice
with no added sugar**

2 tablespoons powdered gelatine

2 teaspoons pure maple syrup

1 Place all the ingredients in a saucepan and whisk until well combined. Stand at room temperature for 5 minutes or until the mixture looks jelly-like.

2 Transfer the pan to medium heat and cook, whisking, until the mixture comes to a simmer and the gelatine has dissolved. Spoon evenly into eighteen 2 teaspoon measure silicon ice-cube moulds.

3 Chill for 4 hours or until set firm. Serve chilled.

PALEO DAIRY FREE GLUTEN FREE REFINED SUGAR FREE LUNCHBOX FRIENDLY

A CUP OF TEA and slice
of DATE LOAF fixes EVERYTHING.

DATE LOAF

SERVES 10 — PREP 15 MINUTES / COOK 1 HOUR 5 MINUTES + COOLING / STAND 10 MINUTES —
TOTAL CALORIES 1634 / CALORIES PER SERVE 163

A very versatile recipe: try having a slice for breakfast with a tablespoon of almond
spread – the spread will add 120 calories along with extra protein.

**8 medjool dates, seeded
and chopped**

3 tablespoons pure maple syrup

3 tablespoons coconut oil

1 teaspoon bicarbonate of soda

2 cups self-raising wholemeal flour

1 teaspoon mixed spice

1 egg, whisked

1 Preheat the oven to 180°C (160°C fan-forced). Line the base and sides
   of an 18 cm × 10 cm loaf tin with baking paper.

2 Place the date, maple syrup, coconut oil and 1 cup cold tap water in a
   large saucepan over high heat. Bring to the boil, then reduce the heat to
   medium and simmer, stirring occasionally, for 3 minutes. Remove the
   pan from the heat and immediately stir in the bicarbonate of soda –
   the mixture will expand and froth up. Cool in the pan for 10 minutes.

3 Add the flour, mixed spice and egg to the date mixture and stir until well
   combined. Spoon the batter into the prepared tin and level the surface.

4 Bake for 1 hour or until golden and a skewer inserted in the centre
   comes out clean. Stand for 10 minutes, then cut into slices and
   serve warm.

VEGETARIAN   DAIRY   REFINED   LUNCHBOX   FREEZER
              FREE   SUGAR FREE   FRIENDLY   FRIENDLY

CHOC-BANANA POPS

MAKES 8 — PREP 10 MINUTES / FREEZE 1 HOUR 5 MINUTES — TOTAL CALORIES 1100 / CALORIES PER SERVE 138

Once you've frozen your bananas, it takes just 10 minutes to make these cute little treats. Wooden pop sticks are easy to find in craft or variety stores.

4 ripe bananas, peeled, halved crossways

2 tablespoons raw cacao powder (see page 296)

1 tablespoon pure maple syrup

2 tablespoons coconut oil, melted

⅔ cup freeze-dried strawberries, crushed

2 tablespoons shredded coconut

1 Line a baking tray with baking paper. Insert a wooden pop stick into the cut end of each banana and place on the prepared tray. Freeze for 1 hour or until firm.

2 Put the cacao powder, maple syrup and coconut oil in a jug and whisk until smooth and well combined. Dip the frozen bananas into the cacao mixture, then immediately sprinkle with crushed strawberry and shredded coconut. Return to the tray and freeze for 5 minutes or until the coating has set firm. Serve frozen.

VEGAN VEGETARIAN   PALEO   DAIRY FREE   GLUTEN FREE   REFINED SUGAR FREE   FREEZER FRIENDLY

Your kids (and you) will NEVER eat a STORE-BOUGHT POP again after these babies.

COCONUT LEMON PUDDING

SERVES 4 — PREP 15 MINUTES / COOK 20 MINUTES / STAND 5 MINUTES —
TOTAL CALORIES 688 / CALORIES PER SERVE 172

Two amazing flavours: coconut and lemon. Yum!

coconut oil or olive oil cooking spray

4 eggs

2 egg yolks

⅓ cup pure maple syrup

1 tablespoon finely grated lemon zest

2 tablespoons fresh lemon juice

½ cup coconut cream

2 teaspoons desiccated coconut

1 Preheat the oven to 160°C (140°C fan-forced). Lightly spray four ¾ cup capacity baking dishes with cooking spray. Place the dishes in a roasting tin, then pour boiling water into the tin to come halfway up the side of the dishes.

2 Place the eggs, egg yolks and maple syrup in a bowl. Using a hand-held mixer, mix on high speed for 3 minutes or until the mixture has quadrupled in volume. Add the lemon zest, lemon juice and coconut cream and whisk briefly until well combined.

3 Pour the pudding mixture evenly into the prepared dishes and carefully transfer to the oven. Bake for 20 minutes or until just set. Remove the puddings from the water bath and stand for just 5 minutes. The puddings will rise and then quickly deflate if they stand for too long after cooking.

4 Sprinkle the tops with coconut and serve warm.

 VEGETARIAN
 PALEO
DAIRY FREE
GLUTEN FREE
REFINED SUGAR FREE

BERRY SORBET

SERVES 4 — PREP 5 MINUTES — TOTAL CALORIES 334 / CALORIES PER SERVE 84

This divine sorbet is best eaten straight away, but leftovers can
be stored in the freezer for up to 6 months.

500 g frozen mixed berries

1 tablespoon fresh lemon juice

1 tablespoon pure maple syrup

1 egg white

1 Place all the ingredients in a high-speed upright blender and blend until completely smooth. Divide among four bowls and serve chilled.

VEGETARIAN   PALEO   DAIRY FREE   GLUTEN FREE   REFINED SUGAR FREE   FREEZER FRIENDLY

LEMON *and* LIME ICE-POPS

Ten minutes to make and totally refreshing.

1 tablespoon finely grated lemon zest

1 tablespoon finely grated lime zest

½ cup fresh lemon juice

½ cup fresh lime juice

½ cup 100 per cent clear apple juice

½ cup small mint leaves

1 Place all the ingredients in a large jug and stir to combine. Pour the mixture evenly into six ½ cup ice-pop moulds and insert wooden pop sticks in the centre.

2 Freeze for 4 hours or until firm. Serve frozen.

VEGAN VEGETARIAN

PALEO

DAIRY FREE

GLUTEN FREE

REFINED SUGAR FREE

FREEZER FRIENDLY

TROPICAL FROZEN YOGHURT

SERVES 6 — PREP 20 MINUTES / FREEZE 2 HOURS — TOTAL CALORIES 1100 / CALORIES PER SERVE 183

This would make the most delicious dessert for a summer dinner party. If you wanted to reduce the calories a bit, it wouldn't hurt to use a low-fat plain yoghurt.

4 ripe bananas, chopped

1 mango, flesh chopped

400 g full-cream Greek yoghurt

4 passionfruit, halved, seeds and juice scraped

1 Line a baking tray with baking paper. Place the banana and mango on the tray in a single layer and freeze for 2 hours or until firm.

2 Transfer the frozen fruit to a high-speed upright blender, add the yoghurt and passionfruit and blend until well combined and completely smooth. Divide among six cups and serve.

The EASIEST,
TASTIEST frozen
dessert you will
EVER make!

VEGETARIAN GLUTEN FREE REFINED SUGAR FREE FREEZER FRIENDLY

CHOC-HAZELNUT FREEZER FUDGE

MAKES 16 PIECES — PREP 15 MINUTES / FREEZE 1 HOUR — TOTAL CALORIES 2138 / CALORIES PER SERVE 134

Raw cacao powder is not the same as cocoa powder, which is full of sugar. Raw cacao is high in antioxidants and is a great mood booster. You'll find it in larger supermarkets. Cacao nibs are available from health-food shops, along with the pure hazelnut spread.

1 cup 100 per cent hazelnut spread

3 tablespoons raw cacao powder

3 tablespoons pure maple syrup

3 tablespoons softened coconut oil

2 tablespoons cacao nibs

2 tablespoons hazelnuts, roasted, skins removed and chopped

1 Line the base and sides of a 20 cm × 10 cm loaf tin with baking paper.

2 Place the hazelnut spread, cacao powder, maple syrup and coconut oil in the bowl of a food processor. Using the pulse button, process until the mixture just comes together. Transfer the mixture to the prepared tin and level the surface, then sprinkle the cacao nibs and hazelnuts over the top, pressing down lightly.

3 Freeze for 1 hour or until almost firm. Cut the fudge into 16 pieces and serve chilled.

VEGAN VEGETARIAN   PALEO   DAIRY FREE   GLUTEN FREE   REFINED SUGAR FREE   FREEZER FRIENDLY

OH SHUT UP!!!

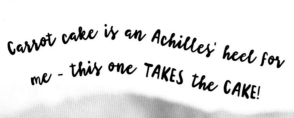

Carrot cake is an Achilles' heel for me - this one TAKES the CAKE!

RAW CARROT CAKE

SERVES 8 — PREP 20 MINUTES / STAND 30 MINUTES / FREEZE 1 HOUR / CHILL 1 HOUR —
TOTAL CALORIES 3809 / CALORIES PER SERVE 476

This is the perfect birthday cake to serve for friends who are vegan, dairy intolerant or gluten intolerant. Anyone with nut allergies needs to BYO.

1 tablespoon walnut halves, roughly chopped

2 tablespoons pumpkin seeds

2 tablespoons flaked coconut

CASHEW-CREAM TOPPING

2 cups raw cashews

boiling water, to cover

½ cup unsweetened almond milk

1 tablespoon pure maple syrup

CARROT CAKE

3 carrots, coarsely grated

1 cup shredded coconut

8 medjool dates, seeded and chopped

½ cup walnut halves

⅓ cup pumpkin seeds

2 teaspoons vanilla bean paste or extract

½ teaspoon ground cinnamon

1. To make the cashew-cream topping, place the cashews in a large heatproof bowl and cover with boiling water. Stand at room temperature for 30 minutes or until softened, then drain and rinse under cold tap water. Transfer to a high-speed upright blender, add the almond milk and maple syrup and blend until smooth. Set aside until needed.

2. Line the base and side of a 20 cm spring-form cake tin with baking paper.

3. For the cake, place all the ingredients in the bowl of a food processor and process until the mixture is finely chopped and holds together when gently pressed. Transfer to the prepared tin and press down firmly to level the surface. Freeze for 1 hour or until set firm.

4. Spread the cashew-cream topping evenly over the cake in the tin and sprinkle with chopped walnuts, pumpkin seeds and flaked coconut. Chill for 1 hour or until the top is almost set. Cut into eight slices and serve chilled.

 VEGAN VEGETARIAN
 PALEO
 DAIRY FREE
 GLUTEN FREE
 REFINED SUGAR FREE
 FREEZER FRIENDLY

I've made these a hundred times over - so, so EASY and just TWO ingredients!

COCONUT WATER *and* RASPBERRY ICE-POPS

MAKES 6 — PREP 15 MINUTES / FREEZE 4 HOURS — TOTAL CALORIES 300 / CALORIES PER SERVE 50

These are not only adorable, they also contain fibre, energy and antioxidants – I can't imagine a better snack for the kids on a hot day.

1 young fresh coconut, opened

125 g raspberries

1 Strain the coconut water from the coconut into a large jug. Using a spoon, scoop out the coconut flesh onto a chopping board. Thinly slice the flesh and add to the coconut water in the jug.

2 Add the raspberries to the coconut mixture and stir to combine. Spoon the mixture evenly into six ½ cup capacity ice-pop moulds and insert wooden pop sticks in the centre. Freeze for 4 hours or until set firm. Serve frozen.

| VEGAN VEGETARIAN | PALEO | DAIRY FREE | GLUTEN FREE | REFINED SUGAR FREE | FREEZER FRIENDLY |

STRAWBERRIES *and* COCO-CREAM

SERVES 4 — PREP 20 MINUTES / STAND 30 MINUTES / CHILL 24 HOURS —
TOTAL CALORIES 1000 / CALORIES PER SERVE 250

The macerated strawberries in this recipe are to die for. Just don't leave them for any longer than 30 minutes, otherwise they'll become too soft.

750 g small strawberries, hulled and halved

1 tablespoon red wine vinegar

1 tablespoon pure maple syrup

COCO-CREAM

1 × 400 ml tin coconut cream

2 teaspoons vanilla bean paste or extract

1 To make the coco-cream, place the tin of coconut cream in the fridge and chill for at least 24 hours. Open the tin and carefully scoop out the thick firm layer of cream that has set on top. Leave the liquid in the base of the tin (use it in your next smoothie). Place the cream in a bowl, add the vanilla and whisk until well combined and soft peaks form. Store in the fridge until needed.

2 Mix together the strawberries, vinegar and maple syrup in a bowl. Stand, covered, at room temperature for 30 minutes to macerate.

3 Divide the strawberry mixture among four bowls or glasses, top with coco-cream and serve.

VEGAN VEGETARIAN   PALEO   DAIRY FREE   GLUTEN FREE   REFINED SUGAR FREE

COCONUT RICE *with* MANGO

SERVES 4 — PREP 10 MINUTES / COOK 5 MINUTES — TOTAL CALORIES 861 / CALORIES PER SERVE 215

Fifteen minutes to heaven.

1 × 165 ml tin light coconut milk

2 tablespoons pure maple syrup

1 cup cooked brown basmati rice (from ½ cup uncooked rice)

½ teaspoon finely grated lime zest

1 mango, cheeks removed, finely sliced

1 tablespoon shredded coconut, toasted

1 Place the coconut milk, maple syrup and rice in a saucepan over medium heat. Stir until the mixture just comes to a simmer and is heated through.

2 Spoon the coconut rice into four bowls, top with the lime zest, mango and shredded coconut and serve warm.

VEGAN
VEGETARIAN

DAIRY
FREE

GLUTEN
FREE

REFINED
SUGAR FREE

Bliss Balls

ORIGINAL

BLISS BALLS

MAKES 12 — PREPARATION 15 MINUTES/ CHILLING 30 MINUTES —
TOTAL CALORIES 1042/ CALORIES PER SERVE 87

The basic recipe for these healthy bliss balls contains just four ingredients.
You can then mix things up by adding bursts of flavour at the rolling stage. Here are my favourite variations.

**12 medjool dates,
seeded and chopped**

⅓ cup unhulled tahini

1 tablespoon chia seeds

½ cup desiccated coconut

1 Line a large baking tray with baking paper.

2 Place the chopped dates, tahini and chia seeds in the bowl of a food
processor and process until well combined and smooth.

3 Roll firmly packed and level tablespoon measures into balls, then roll
the balls in the coconut to coat. Place on the prepared tray and chill
for 30 minutes. Serve chilled, or store in an airtight container in the
fridge for up to 2 weeks or in the freezer for up to 2 months.

VARIATIONS

STRAWBERRY:
Finely crush ⅔ cup of freeze-dried strawberries
and add to the desiccated coconut before rolling.

ZESTY:
Add 2 teaspoons each of finely grated lemon
zest, lime zest and orange zest to the desiccated
coconut before rolling.

CACAO:
Add 3 teaspoons of raw cacao powder (see page
296) to the desiccated coconut before rolling.

PISTACHIO:
Add 2 tablespoons of finely chopped pistachio
kernels to the desiccated coconut before rolling.

SPICED SWEET PUMPKIN SCONES

MAKES 12 — PREP 20 MINUTES + COOLING / COOK 15 MINUTES —
TOTAL CALORIES 1250 / CALORIES PER SERVE 104

These scones are delicious for morning tea, especially when served
with the Strawberry Chia Jam on page 89.

1 cup warm mashed pumpkin

25 g butter

2 tablespoons pure maple syrup

1 egg, whisked

½ teaspoon mixed spice

**1½ cups wholemeal
self-raising flour**

½ cup fresh full-cream ricotta

**½ cup Strawberry Chia Jam
(see page 89)**

1 Preheat the oven to 200°C (180°C fan-forced) and line a baking tray
with baking paper.

2 Place the warm pumpkin in a heatproof bowl, add the butter and
stir until the butter has melted and the mixture is well combined.
Cool to room temperature.

3 Add the maple syrup, egg and mixed spice to the pumpkin mixture and
stir until smooth, then stir in the flour until just combined.

4 Drop dessertspoonfuls of dough onto the prepared tray, spaced about
3 cm apart. Bake for 15 minutes or until light golden and cooked (the
bases should sound hollow when tapped).

5 Split the warm scones, top with ricotta and jam and serve warm.

VEGETARIAN   PALEO   REFINED SUGAR FREE   LUNCHBOX FRIENDLY   FREEZER FRIENDLY

SALTED CARAMEL SLICE

MAKES 20 PIECES — PREP 20 MINUTES / FREEZE 1 HOUR 10 MINUTES / STAND 5 MINUTES —
TOTAL CALORIES 4990 / CALORIES PER SERVE 250

Melt-in-the-mouth delicious, but pretty heavy on the calories, so keep this
one for special occasions. Freeze some slices in individual zip-locks if you
like, to help you resist temptation!

1 cup raw macadamias

½ cup desiccated coconut

⅓ cup softened coconut oil

½ teaspoon sea salt flakes

SALTED CARAMEL

½ cup softened coconut oil

⅓ cup unhulled tahini

⅓ cup pure maple syrup

3 tablespoons coconut milk

3 tablespoons almond spread

**1 teaspoon vanilla bean paste
or extract**

½ teaspoon sea salt flakes

TOPPING

½ cup softened coconut oil

**3 tablespoons raw cacao powder
(see page 296)**

1 tablespoon pure maple syrup

1 Line the base and sides of a 20 cm square cake tin with baking paper.

2 Place the macadamias, desiccated coconut and coconut oil in the
bowl of a food processor and process until finely chopped and well
combined. Press the mixture firmly into the base of the prepared tin
and freeze for 20 minutes.

3 To make the salted caramel, put all the ingredients in a high-speed
upright blender and blend until smooth. Pour the mixture over the
macadamia base in the tin and level the surface. Freeze for 30 minutes
or until almost firm.

4 For the topping, place all the ingredients in a bowl and whisk until
smooth and well combined. Pour over the salted caramel in the tin
and level the surface. Return to the freezer for a further 20 minutes
or until almost firm.

5 Transfer the slice to a chopping board. Stand for 5 minutes to soften
slightly, then cut into 20 pieces. Serve chilled, sprinkled with sea salt.

VEGAN
VEGETARIAN   PALEO   DAIRY
FREE   GLUTEN
FREE   REFINED
SUGAR FREE   FREEZER
FRIENDLY

Two words: SALTED CARAMEL. All done.

SLOW-COOKER SPICED PEARS

SERVES 4 — PREP 10 MINUTES / COOK 4 HOURS — TOTAL CALORIES 542 / CALORIES PER SERVE 136

If you love slow-cooked treats, you'll love this super-easy option.
They are so great on brekkie porridge too.

4 pears, peeled

2 cinnamon sticks

3 star anise

1.5 litres boiling water

3 tablespoons pure maple syrup

1 Place all the ingredients in a slow cooker. Cook on high for 4 hours or until the pears are tender.

2 Divide the pears among four bowls and spoon over the poaching liquid. Serve warm.

VEGAN VEGETARIAN   PALEO   DAIRY FREE   GLUTEN FREE   REFINED SUGAR FREE

Put these on before
bedtime and wake up to
a DELICIOUS-SMELLING house.

APPLE *and* RASPBERRY FILO STACKS

SERVES 4 — PREP 25 MINUTES / COOK 15 MINUTES / STAND 3 MINUTES —
TOTAL CALORIES 536 / CALORIES PER SERVE 134

A delicate dessert that's quite low in calories.

2 sheets filo pastry

1 tablespoon pure maple syrup

coconut oil cooking spray

2 small red apples, very finely sliced, seeded

150 g raspberries, torn in half

¼ teaspoon ground cardamom

⅓ cup Labne (see page 330)

1 Preheat the oven to 200°C (180°C fan-forced). Line two large baking trays with baking paper.

2 Lay the filo sheets out flat on a clean work surface. Brush with maple syrup and spray lightly with cooking spray, then stack on top of each other, syrup-side up. Cut the filo stack lengthways into three pieces, then cut each length crossways into four pieces.

3 Transfer the filo pieces to the prepared trays, top with the apple and raspberries and sprinkle with cardamom. Bake for 15 minutes or until the pastry is crisp underneath and golden. Stand for 3 minutes on the trays.

4 Stack three pastries on each of four plates and serve warm with labne.

VEGETARIAN   REFINED SUGAR FREE

STRAWBERRY COCONUT PIE

SERVES 8 — PREP 15 MINUTES / COOK 35 MINUTES / STAND 10 MINUTES —
TOTAL CALORIES 1902 / CALORIES PER SERVE 238

An overload of deliciousness.

3 tablespoons macadamia oil

3 eggs

3 tablespoons pure maple syrup

½ cup almond meal

3 tablespoons self-raising wholemeal flour

1 cup desiccated coconut

2 × 165 ml tins light coconut milk

250 g small strawberries, hulled and halved

1 Preheat the oven to 180°C (160°C fan-forced). Use a little of the oil to grease a 22 cm glass pie plate.

2 Place the remaining oil in a bowl with the eggs, maple syrup, almond meal, flour, coconut and coconut milk and whisk until smooth and well combined. Pour the batter into the prepared pie plate and arrange the strawberries over the top.

3 Bake for 35 minutes or until golden and a skewer inserted in the centre comes out clean. Stand for 10 minutes, then serve warm.

VEGETARIAN   DAIRY FREE   REFINED SUGAR FREE

CACAO MOUSSE *with* PEAR

Yes, a guilt-free treat.

1 small avocado, flesh chopped

2 overripe bananas

3 tablespoons raw cacao powder (see page 296)

2 tablespoons pure maple syrup

½ teaspoon mixed spice

1 tablespoon vanilla bean paste or extract

2 large pears, cored and cut into wedges

1 Place the avocado, banana, cacao, maple syrup, mixed spice and vanilla in a high-speed upright blender and blend until smooth.

2 Pour the mixture into four glasses and chill for 1 hour. Top with the pear wedges and serve chilled.

VEGAN VEGETARIAN PALEO DAIRY FREE GLUTEN FREE REFINED SUGAR FREE

ROCKY ROAD BITES

MAKES 18 — PREP 10 MINUTES / CHILL 30 MINUTES — TOTAL CALORIES 885 / CALORIES PER SERVE 49

The perfect snack with an afternoon cuppa (as long as you can stop at one).

⅓ cup raw cacao powder (see page 296), plus ½ teaspoon extra

3 tablespoons softened coconut oil

25 g mini marshmallows

1 cup puffed rice

3 tablespoons craisins

2 tablespoons shredded coconut

1 tablespoon pure maple syrup

1 Line a large baking tray with baking paper.

2 Place all the ingredients in a large bowl and stir gently until well combined. Drop tablespoons of mixture in mounds on the prepared tray, then chill for 30 minutes or until set firm. Dust with extra cacao powder and serve chilled.

VEGAN VEGETARIAN   DAIRY FREE   GLUTEN FREE   FREEZER FRIENDLY

This is a TOP-SHELF TREAT, with kid-friendly melt-and-mix preparation.

RAW BANOFFEE PIE

SERVES 12 — PREP 25 MINUTES / CHILL 30 MINUTES / COOK 5 MINUTES + COOLING —
TOTAL CALORIES 3525 / CALORIES PER SERVE 294

A way more nutritious version of the traditional pie, though it
still packs a calorie punch, so keep it for a special occasion.

1½ cups raw cashews

½ cup desiccated coconut

8 medjool dates, seeded
and chopped

3 tablespoons coconut
oil, melted

¼ teaspoon mixed spice

2 bananas, finely sliced

2 tablespoons fresh lemon juice

1 quantity Coco-cream
(see page 302)

20 g dark chocolate (70 per cent
cocoa), finely chopped

FILLING

12 medjool dates, seeded
and chopped

1 × 165 ml tin light coconut milk

2 teaspoons vanilla bean paste
or extract

1 To make the filling, put all the ingredients in a high-speed upright
blender and blend until smooth. Pour the mixture into a small
saucepan and bring to a simmer over medium heat. Simmer, stirring
constantly, for 3 minutes or until the mixture thickens and turns deep
golden. Remove from the heat and cool to room temperature in the pan.

2 Meanwhile, place the cashews in the bowl of a food processor and
process until very finely chopped. Add the desiccated coconut, dates,
oil and mixed spice and process until well combined and slightly sticky.
Add 1–2 tablespoons water if necessary to bring the mixture together.
Press evenly and firmly over the base and side of a 20 cm pie plate.
Chill for 30 minutes or until set firm.

3 Place the banana and lemon juice in a bowl and toss gently to combine.

4 Spoon the filling over the cashew base and level the surface.
Layer the banana slices over the filling, then spread the coco-cream
over the top and finish with a sprinkling of chocolate. Cut into
12 slices. Serve immediately or chill for up to 4 hours.

*A SECRET: the caterers on The Biggest
Loser would occasionally make banoffee
pie as a treat for the staff and crew - well,
it was SO DAMN GOOD that there would
be a SCRAMBLE to get a piece! This
version trumps that and more!*

VEGETARIAN   GLUTEN
FREE   REFINED
SUGAR FREE

CHOC-HAZELNUT CUPS

MAKES 24 — PREP 15 MINUTES / CHILL 30 MINUTES — TOTAL CALORIES 2026 / CALORIES PER SERVE 84

Perfectly portioned treats.

½ cup coconut oil

½ cup raw cacao powder (see page 296)

½ cup 100 per cent hazelnut spread

3 tablespoons pure maple syrup

2 teaspoons vanilla bean paste or extract

1 Line a 24-hole mini muffin tin with paper cases.

2 Place all the ingredients in a high-speed upright blender and blend until well combined and completely smooth.

3 Spoon the chocolate mixture evenly into the paper cases and level the surface. Chill for 30 minutes or until softly set. Serve straight away, or store in an airtight container in the fridge for up to 1 week or in the freezer for up to 3 months.

VEGAN VEGETARIAN

PALEO

DAIRY FREE

GLUTEN FREE

REFINED SUGAR FREE

FREEZER FRIENDLY

BAKED CHOC-RASPBERRY PUDDINGS

SERVES 4 — PREP 15 MINUTES / COOK 10 MINUTES — TOTAL CALORIES 852 / CALORIES PER SERVE 213

Go for a minimum of 70 per cent cocoa chocolate here – 80 per cent is even better!

50 g butter, melted

50 g dark chocolate (70 per cent cocoa), finely chopped

3 eggs, whisked

2 tablespoons pure maple syrup

½ cup wholemeal self-raising flour

150 g raspberries

1 Preheat the oven to 160°C (140°C fan-forced). Place a baking tray in the oven to heat. Use a little of the melted butter to grease four ¾ cup capacity ramekins.

2 Place the butter, chocolate, egg, maple syrup and flour in a bowl and stir until well combined. Gently fold in the raspberries. Spoon the mixture into the prepared ramekins and level the surface.

3 Place the ramekins on the preheated tray in the oven and bake for 10 minutes or until firm around edges and slightly soft in the centre. Stand for 2 minutes, then serve warm.

VEGETARIAN   REFINED SUGAR FREE

BEETROOT FUDGE BROWNIES

MAKES 16 — PREP 15 MINUTES / COOK 40 MINUTES / REST 10 MINUTES —
TOTAL CALORIES 1589 / CALORIES PER SERVE 99

No one will ever guess there's a hidden superfood in these brownies. The beetroot adds
moisture and sweetness as well as nutritional goodness.

3 tablespoons coconut oil, melted

½ cup raw cacao powder
(see page 296)

3 tablespoons pure maple syrup

½ cup unsweetened apple puree

2 teaspoons vanilla bean paste
or extract

2 eggs, whisked

1 beetroot, coarsely grated

¾ cup almond meal

⅓ cup desiccated coconut

2 teaspoons pure icing sugar, sifted

1 Preheat the oven to 160°C (140°C fan-forced) and line the base and
   sides of a 20 cm square cake tin with baking paper.

2 Place the oil, cacao powder, maple syrup, apple puree, vanilla, egg,
   beetroot, almond meal and 3 tablespoons desiccated coconut in
   a bowl and stir until well combined. Spoon the mixture into the
   prepared tin and level the surface. Bake for 40 minutes or until the
   edges have set and the centre is still slightly soft. Rest for 10 minutes.

3 Combine the icing sugar and remaining coconut in a bowl. Transfer
   the brownie to a serving plate and sprinkle with the coconut mixture.
   Cut into 16 pieces and serve warm.

VEGETARIAN   DAIRY FREE   GLUTEN FREE   LUNCHBOX FRIENDLY FREEZER FRIENDLY

It's TRUE - a healthy cheesecake DOES exist!

PASSIONFRUIT CHEESECAKE POTS

SERVES 4 — PREP 15 MINUTES / CHILL 30 MINUTES — TOTAL CALORIES 531 / CALORIES PER SERVE 133

A lovely light dessert – looks so indulgent yet is not bad on the calorie front.

3 tablespoons light spreadable cream cheese

100 g fresh full-cream ricotta

3 tablespoons Labne (see page 333)

4 passionfruit, halved, seeds and juice scraped

1 tablespoon pure maple syrup

1 tablespoon pistachio kernels, finely chopped

1   Place the cream cheese and ricotta in a bowl. Using a hand-held mixer, mix on high speed for 2 minutes or until smooth.

2   Add the labne and passionfruit and mix until well combined. Divide the mixture among four ¾ cup capacity serving glasses or jars and chill for 30 minutes.

3   Top the cheesecake pots with maple syrup and chopped pistachio and serve chilled.

VEGETARIAN   PALEO   GLUTEN FREE   REFINED SUGAR FREE

VANILLA CUPCAKES

MAKES 12 — PREP 25 MINUTES / COOK 15 MINUTES + COOLING —
TOTAL CALORIES 1090 / CALORIES PER SERVE 91

The ricotta icing on these lovely cupcakes is best made with full-cream ricotta cut from
a block from a deli – the ricotta in tubs is much wetter and will make your icing sloppy.

1½ cups wholemeal
self-raising flour

1 cup unsweetened apple puree

1 egg, whisked

1 tablespoon pure maple syrup

2 teaspoons vanilla bean paste
or extract

125 g blueberries

RICOTTA ICING

100 g fresh full-cream ricotta

3 tablespoons unsweetened
apple puree

1 tablespoon pure maple syrup

½ teaspoon vanilla bean paste
or extract

1 Preheat the oven to 180°C (160°C fan-forced) and line a 12-hole,
⅓ cup capacity muffin tin with paper cases.

2 Place the flour, apple puree, egg, maple syrup and vanilla in
a bowl and stir until just combined – do not overmix otherwise the
cakes will be tough. Spoon the batter into the paper cases.

3 Bake for 15 minutes or until golden and a skewer inserted in the
centre comes out clean. Cool in the tin for 5 minutes, then transfer
to a wire rack to cool completely.

4 To make the icing, put all the ingredients in a bowl. Using a hand-
held mixer, mix on high speed for 2 minutes or until smooth and
well combined.

5 Spread the ricotta icing over the cooled cupcakes and top with
blueberries. These are best enjoyed on the day they are made.

VEGETARIAN   REFINED   FREEZER
              SUGAR FREE FRIENDLY

We've done it – a HEALTHY CUPCAKE! The cookbook
wouldn't be right without one after all ...

Basics

TOMATO PASSATA

MAKES 1 LITRE (8 SERVES) — PREP 20 MINUTES / COOK 35 MINUTES —
TOTAL CALORIES 366 / CALORIES PER SERVE 46

Make your own veggie-packed tomato passata and you'll never go back
to the shop-bought version.

2 onions, chopped

2 garlic cloves, chopped

2 celery stalks, chopped

1 carrot, chopped

1 kg very ripe tomatoes, chopped

1 red capsicum, seeded and chopped

½ cup basil leaves

1 Place the onion, garlic, celery, carrot and 3 tablespoons cold tap water in a large saucepan over high heat. Cover and cook, stirring occasionally, for 10 minutes or until the vegetables are very tender and just starting to colour.

2 Add the tomato and capsicum and cook, covered and stirring occasionally, for 5 minutes or until the tomato just starts to collapse.

3 Pour in 1 litre water. Bring to the boil, then reduce the heat to low and cook, covered, for 20 minutes or until the mixture is very soft and slightly reduced.

4 Remove the pan from the heat, then stir in the basil and season to taste. Using a hand-held blender, blend until the mixture is smooth.

5 Use straight away or cool to room temperature and store in an airtight container in the fridge for up to 1 week, or freeze in airtight containers for up to 6 months.

CHICKEN STOCK

MAKES 5 LITRES (20 SERVES) — PREP 15 MINUTES / COOK 1 HOUR —
TOTAL CALORIES 1466 / CALORIES PER SERVE 73

The leftover chicken here is great for burritos, lunchtime wraps, in salads or tossed through your favourite stir-fried vegetables. Pull away all of the cooked chicken meat from the bones, cool to room temperature then store in an airtight container in the fridge for up to 3 days or freeze for up to 3 months.

1 × 1.6 kg chicken, wiped clean

1 bunch flat-leaf parsley, torn in half

2 large carrots, chopped

2 onions, chopped

4 large celery stalks, chopped

2 dried bay leaves

1 teaspoon black peppercorns

1   Place the chicken, breast-side down, in a large stockpot and add the remaining ingredients. Pour in 6 litres cold tap water.

2   Bring to the boil over high heat, then reduce the heat to low and simmer, partially covered and occasionally skimming the surface of any impurities, for 1 hour or until the chicken is very tender and falls apart easily when tested with tongs.

3   Remove the pot from the heat and carefully transfer the chicken to a large heatproof bowl. Strain the stock mixture into large heatproof bowls, discarding the solids.

4   Use straight away or cool to room temperature and store in airtight containers in the fridge for up to 1 week, or freeze for up to 3 months.

VARIATIONS:

Vegetable stock: swap the chicken for 1 kg mixed vegetables, such as pumpkin, sweet potato, parsnip, celeriac, swede, turnip and leek.

Fish stock: swap the chicken for 1 kg clean fish bones and heads. Reduce the simmering time to 30 minutes to prevent the stock from tasting bitter.

Beef stock: swap the chicken for 1.5 kg beef soup bones. Increase the simmering time to 3 hours, topping up with extra boiling water as needed.

FERMENTED SLAW

MAKES 3 CUPS (ABOUT 36 SERVES) — PREP 20 MINUTES / STAND 4–7 DAYS —
TOTAL CALORIES 398 / CALORIES PER SERVE 11

Enjoy 2 tablespoons of fermented slaw with every meal
to improve your gut flora.

**300 g red cabbage,
finely shredded**

**300 g green cabbage,
finely shredded**

1 zucchini, coarsely grated

2 carrots, coarsely grated

**4 spring onions, halved lengthways,
then cut into 3 cm lengths**

1 tablespoon yellow mustard seeds

2 tablespoons sea salt flakes

1 Place all the ingredients in a very large bowl. Using clean hands, firmly massage and squeeze the mixture together for 10 minutes or until the vegetables have softened and their natural juices have been released.

2 Firmly pack the vegetable mixture and all the released juices into a 750 ml sterilised glass jar (see note below), making sure that the juice covers the top of the vegetables completely. Leave at least a 2 cm gap between the top of the vegetable mixture and the lid (this will allow room for the fermentation). Seal the jar.

3 Stand the jar at room temperature, away from direct sunlight, for 4–7 days. You should notice the mixture starting to bubble after the first 2 days, but the exact timing will depend on the warmth of your kitchen.

4 Taste your slaw on day 4: if it is to your liking, start using it straight away and store in the fridge for up to 1 month. If you prefer your slaw to have extra zing, continue to ferment at room temperature for up to 7 days, tasting each day to see how it is progressing.

NOTE:

Sterilising jars: rinse the jars, lids and rubber seals in very hot soapy water to clean well, then rinse under hot running water until all the soap scum has been removed. Place the jars and lids (not rubber seals) on a baking tray and into a 120°C (100°C fan-forced) oven for 20 minutes or until completely dry. Cool on the tray before filling.

LABNE

MAKES ¾ CUP LABNE (9 SERVES) / MAKES ½ CUP WHEY — PREP 10 MINUTES / CHILL 12–24 HOURS —
TOTAL CALORIES 703 / CALORIES PER SERVE 78

You can buy muslin from fabric stores, some large supermarkets and kitchenware
shops. Refrain from using a clean tea towel as these are treated with dyes.

500 g full-cream Greek yoghurt

1 teaspoon sea salt flakes

1 Place the yoghurt and salt in a bowl and stir until well combined.

2 Line a colander with a large doubled piece of muslin. Set the colander
   over a large bowl, making sure the base of the colander clears the base
   of the bowl by at least 5 cm.

3 Spoon the yoghurt mixture into the muslin, then gather the muslin
   ends, twisting to knot tightly.

4 Place in the fridge for 12–24 hours or until all of the whey has been
   released and the yoghurt has become very thick and firm.

5 Use the labne straight away or store it in an airtight container in
   the fridge for up to 1 week. The leftover whey will keep in an airtight
   container in the fridge for up to 1 week or freeze for up to 3 months.
   The whey can be added to smoothies, pancake, pikelet, cake or muffin
   batters, soups or scrambled eggs.

VARIATIONS:

Savoury: stir in freshly chopped soft herbs (tarragon, chives, parsley,
basil or coriander), finely chopped chilli or garlic, or grated fresh ginger.

Sweet: stir in freshly chopped fruit, pureed or crushed berries, poached
or roasted fruit or a little honey and some sweet spices (ground cinnamon,
mixed spice, nutmeg or ginger).

ACKNOWLEDGEMENTS

I would like to thank everybody who has helped make this book a reality. A big thanks to my team, Gisi, Alex and Peta, for their hard work, and to my management team at Chic for all their support over the years: Jane Weston, Joseph Hanrahan and Ursula Hufnagl.

I am very grateful for the great work by my new publishing team at Pan Mac, especially Ingrid Ohlsson for her drive, dedication and belief in me, as well as Ariane Durkin, Tracey Pattison and Miriam Cannell who were all so committed to this project. A big thank you also to Rob Palmer, Trisha Garner, Grace West, Michelle Noerianto, Simone Forte, Lucia Arias-Martinez and Naomi van Groll.

Finally I'd like to dedicate this book to my son, Axe, the centre of my world.

Mish xxx

A

adrenaline, impact on health 53

alcohol *see* drinks

almonds *see* nuts

Almost nicoise salad 144

amino acids 26, 30

antioxidants in fruit 23

apples 23

Apple nut butter
sandwiches 263

artificial sweeteners, reducing
intake of 43

asparagus 17

Gingered kale and asparagus
stir-fry with sichuan beef 166

atherosclerosis 13, 42

autoimmune diseases
due to fat 12

avocado 17

Avo smash with beetroot 236

Garlic mushrooms and dukkah
avocado 108

Kiwi and avocado smoothie 87

B

bacon

Roast winter vegetable and bacon
soup 133

Spinach and fennel pikelets with
bacon 122

Baked choc-raspberry puddings 321

Baked herb ricotta 239

Baked porridge 77

Baked ratatouille eggs 102

bananas

Apple and raspberry filo
stacks 312

Banana maple french toast 91

Banana pancakes with pineapple
and strawberry salsa 78

Blueberry and banana
smoothie 87

Choc-banana pops 288

Raw banoffee pie 319

barbecuing 204–205

Basics 329–333

beans *see* legumes

Multi-purpose frittata 115

beef

Beef and beetroot on rye 168

Beef stock 331

Garlic mushrooms, celeriac
smash and peppered steak 189

Gingered kale and asparagus
stir-fry with sichuan beef 166

Mexican black beans 227

beetroot 17

Avo smash with beetroot 236

Beef and beetroot on rye 168

Beetroot fudge brownies 323

Broccoli and lamb kofta with
herby beetroot salad 200

Sumac roasted beets and
tomatoes with fried egg 111

berries 23 *see also*
raspberries; strawberries

Baked porridge 77

Berry sorbet 292

Blueberry and banana smoothie
87

Cranberry jelly lollies 285

Rosewater citrus and berries
with yoghurt 80

beverages *see* drinks

biodynamic foods 14

biscuits *see* cookies

black beans *see* beans

blood pressure 35, 42

blueberries *see* berries

bok choy 17

bread, wraps and rolls 28
see also loaves

Banana maple french toast 91

Beef and beetroot on rye 168

Burger builder 171

Chicken caesar wrap 156

Fattoush with salmon 213

The new pizza 190–193

Yoghurt flatbreads 117

breakfast 41, 75–123

Breakfast greens with spiced
chickpeas 121

broccoli 17

Broccoli and lamb kofta with
herby beetroot salad 200

Cauliflower and broccoli fried
'rice' 151

Cauliflower and broccoli
popcorn 249

The new pizza 192–193

No-cook stir-through pasta
sauces 216

Stir-fried broccoli and cashew
chicken 202

broccolini 17, 205

brownies

Beetroot fudge brownies 323

Brussels sprouts 17, 204

Citrus couscous with brussels
sprouts 169

Dill-pickled mushrooms and
glazed sprouts 113

Fluffy omelette with brussels
sprouts 149

Sprouts and peas with lemon
pepper squid 176

Burger builder 170–171

butter 33

Butter bean and tomato soup 132

C

cabbage 17–18, 20

Chinese cabbage wraps 154

Fermented slaw 332

Cacao chilli nuts 235

Cacao mousse with pear 315

cacao nibs

Choc-hazelnut freezer fudge 296

caffeine 37, 52

Cajun roast pumpkin and quinoa
salad 157

cakes, muffins and scones

Earl grey and lemon syrup
muffin bites 84

Raw carrot cake 299

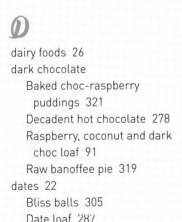

During her 25 years in the health and fitness industry, Michelle Bridges has focused on breaking down the barriers that block the path to a happier and healthier life. Her highly successful 12 Week Body Transformation is Australia's top online exercise and mindset program, and has helped Australians lose more than 1.5 million kilos. She is the bestselling author of 13 books on nutrition and fitness, including *Food for Life*.

First published 2016 in Macmillan
by Pan Macmillan Australia Pty Limited
1 Market Street, Sydney, New South Wales,
Australia 2000

Text copyright © Michelle Bridges
Photography copyright © Rob Palmer
Illustrations copyright © Trisha Garner

A CIP catalogue record for this book is available from the National Library of Australia:
http://catalogue.nla.gov.au

Design by Trisha Garner
Additional design by Grace West
Photography by Rob Palmer
Prop and food styling by Michelle Noerianto
Recipe development by Tracey Pattison
Nutritional analysis by Marieke Rodenstein
Editing by Miriam Cannell and Rachel Carter
Fashion styling by Lucia Arias-Martinez
Makeup by Simone Forte
Colour + reproduction by Splitting Image
Printed in China by Imago Productions

IMPRINT